All **You** Should **Know** About

BREASTFEEDING

All **You** Should **Know** About

BREASTFEEDING

Parvesh Handa

PEACOCK BOOKS

Published by
PEACOCK BOOKS
7/22, Ansari Road, Darya Ganj, New Delhi-110 002
Phones : 2327 3880, 2327 5880, 2328 0451
Fax : +91-11-2328 5873
E-mail : info@atlanticbooks.com
Web : www.atlanticbooks.com

Branch Office
5, Nallathambi Street, Wallajah Road,
Chennai-600 002
Phones : +91-44-6461 1085, 3241 3319
E-mail : chennai@atlanticbooks.com

Peacock Books is an imprint of
Atlantic Publishers and Distributors (P) Ltd.

Printed in India at Nice Printing Press, A-33/3A, Site-IV, Industrial Area, Sahibabad, Ghaziabad, U.P.

This book is lovingly dedicated to
respected Guru Dev

(Dr.) Pt. Manmohan Sashtri Ji
of Babyal (Ambala)

for his constant Gifts of Light, Life,
Inspirations and Divine True Love

Sincere gratitude for the exceptional cooperation and contributions for assisting in preparing this book to

Dr. D.S. Jaspal
President
Indian Medical Association, Haryana

Dr. Suresh Sharma
MD (Obs & Gynae)
Haryana Civil Medical Services, Haryana

Dr. Rajeev Gupta
MD (Radiology)
PGI MS, Rohtak

Preface

Breastfeeding is one of the most exciting, memorable and enjoyable experiences for a woman. But, unfortunately there are yet many women who have not kept up with new research findings about the nutritional and immunological advantages of human milk for infants. In the recent years, there has been an explosion of research into the properties of breast milk, the value of nursing for both mothers and infants, and also the practices that enhance or hinder the course of breastfeeding. It has been unanimously acknowledged by all medical experts as well as researches that there is nothing as good as breast milk for the newborns. What is exactly required of nursing mother is the skill of easy breastfeeding.

In the present book, an attempt has been made to provide the latest expert advice on everything a mother ought to know to make nursing a deeply rewarding part of her life. A complete nursing mother's companion, the book provides authoritative details in the basics of nursing—proper positioning of the baby for nursing, enhancing milk supply, expressing milk by hand as well as pumps, night feedings, successful breastfeeding for working mothers, etc.; issues facing nursing moms; diet and nutrition; measures to be taken before the baby arrives; exercises (yoga) and fitness to name a few. Apart from these, the book gives useful tips on wardrobe and beauty that need to be taken care of during pregnancy and nursing. Above all, it acquaints with breast disorders and diseases and their related surgery. A detailed chapter on mammography is of particular importance for women of all ages. A skilful blend of professional expertise and practical advice, this well-illustrated book will prove highly valuable health guide to all concerned with breastfeeding and maintaining of healthy breast.

I owe a debt of gratitude to all those persons and medical practitioners who have extended their valuable advice and cooperation in the preparation of this book.

PARVESH HANDA

Contents

1

The Breast and Breastfeeding

The breast occupies the space between the second or third and the sixth or seventh ribs and between the sternum and the midaxillary line. Breast tissue may also extend into the anterior axillary fold along the margin of the insertion of the pectoralis major muscle. Beneath the breast is a thin layer of fibrous connective tissue through which lymphatic extensions pervade the underlying muscles. The glandular tissue lies upon this pectoral fascia and, to a lesser extent, upon a similar layer overlying the serratus anterior muscle. The blood supply is from three sources: the anterior aortic intercostals, the internal mammary artery, and the thoracoacromial trunk of the axillary artery. The areola is a circular pigmented patch of skin, 3-5 cm in diameter, overlying the centre of the breast and surrounding the nipple (Fig. 1.1). On its surface are many small rounded elevations indicating the presence of sebaceous glands, which lubricate the nipple during lactation. The nipple consists of erectile tissue surrounding the ductal network that delivers milk at the time of lactation. Both nipple and areola are rich in blood vessels and lymphatics. Beneath the

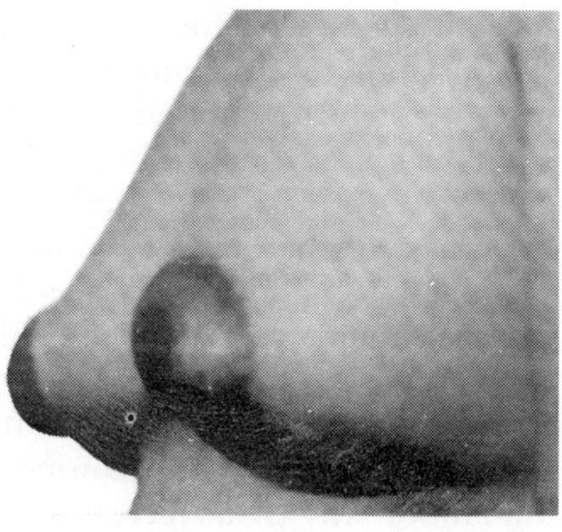

Fig. 1.1. Developing breasts

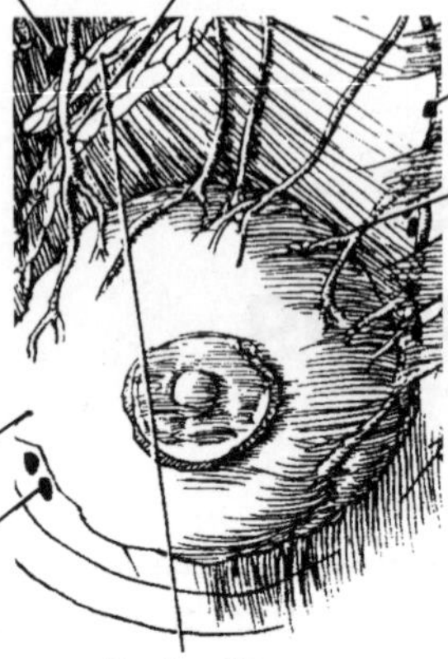

Fig. 1.2. Lymphatics and blood supply of the breasts

skin is a fatty subcutaneous tissue investing the glandular parenchyma of the breast which assists in supporting both glandular and fatty elements. This connective tissue also forms a network for blood vessels and lymphatics (Fig. 1.2) and maintains breast contour which consists of 15 or 20 lobes of varying size and roughly pyramidal shape, radiating from the nipple and lying close to the under surface of the corium throughout the breast (Fig. 1.3). Each lobe has its own excretory duct. The lobes are subdivided further by connective tissue into lobules. As the ducts approach the nipple, they enlarge, forming a sinus or reservoir, which temporarily holds the secretions of the gland. Each duct is surrounded by a column of connective tissues that connect directly with the overlying skin. Fatty tissue comprises a large part of the bulk of the breast (Fig. 1.4). The breasts of prepubertal children consist entirely of ducts and connective tissues. At puberty, rudimentary gland buds increase in size and proliferate, the first manifestation of which is a symmetrical palpable enlargement or bud beneath the nipple. Full development requires about 4 years. During the reproductive years, the amount of fatty tissue increases, along with the development of the lobular structure, and the proportion of fat to glandular

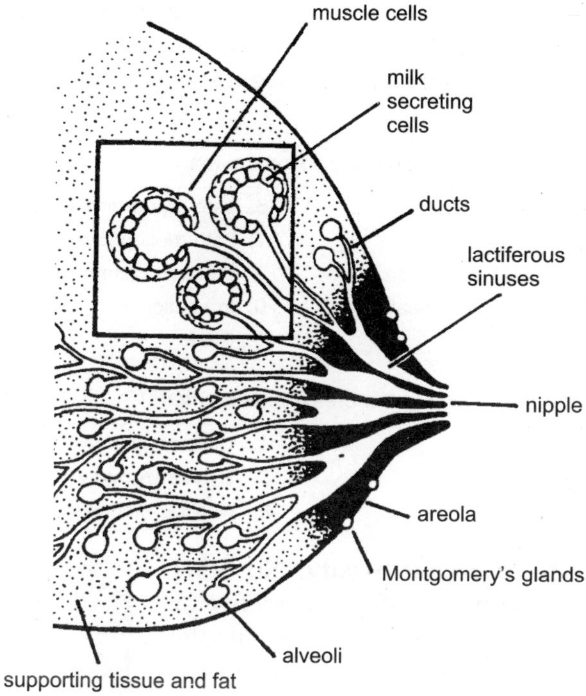

Fig. 1.3. Topography of the breast

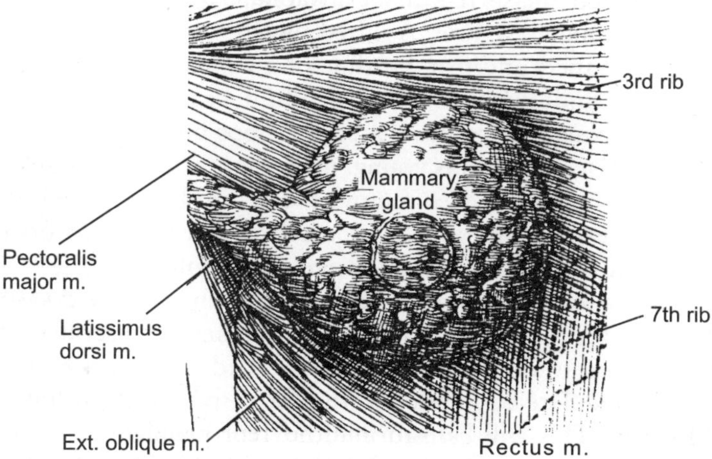

Fig. 1.4. Topography of the breast

tissue has a significant effect on the size and consistency of the breast and the clarity of mammographic studies. Factors affecting risk of breast diseases and their diagnostic aids are shown below in Tables 1 & 2:

Table 1: Risk factors predisposing to carcinoma

1. Family history	6. Late age at first childbirth
2. Advancing age	7. Late menopause
3. Carcinoma in other breast	8. Western culture
4. Precancerous mastopathy	9. Irradiation
5. Early puberty	10. Other

Table 2: Diagnostic aids in the breast management

1. Mammography	4. Ultrasonography
2. Xeroradiography	5. Diaphanography
3. Thermography	6. Nuclear magnetic resonance

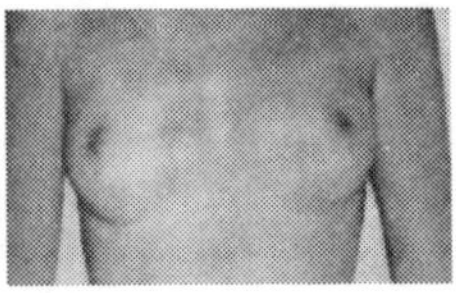

Fig. 1.5. A teenage girl with well developing breasts

Secrets of breast beauty: No other part of a woman's body is as attractive or enjoying as supreme a position as the breast. The first thing that attracts an onlooker is the bustline of a passing woman (Fig. 1.5). Shapeless, small, sluggish or overdeveloped breasts reduce the attraction of a streamlined figure. A lifted, well-rounded, shapely and firm bustline of a woman gives her added attractions and symbolises the youthful beauty of a woman. With the passage of youth, the bust droops but if this begins to happen when a woman is young, immediate attention should be paid to minimize and even remove the defect. Breast care is very important especially for feeding mother. If a woman's breasts get dry and flabby at an early age, they will fail to give the necessary sexual pleasure. It has been rightly said by doctor—"What is the use of breasts which are neither useful to the husband, nor to the child." To cure mottled-looking skin on the breasts, stimulate circulation with alternative rinses of hot and cold water. This will help to minimize the problems and make your bosom firmer. If the skin looks wrinkled and sagging (usually after childbirth or breastfeeding), use a good moisturizing cream. In case the delivery was normal, after about 15 days, a woman can start doing a few light exercises. When breasts lose shape in the twenties this can become a matter of great worry. It is necessary to specify whether the woman in question is a feeding mother. Breasts start sagging and losing their tautness after delivery or during a long illness, during pregnancy or because of irregular menstruation.

IMPORTANT TERMS FOR FEEDING THE BABY

Exclusive breastfeeding: Exclusive breastfeeding means giving a baby no other food or drink, including no water, in addition to breastfeeding (except medicines and vitamin or mineral drops; expressed breast milk is also permitted).

Predominant breastfeeding: Predominant breastfeeding means breastfeeding a baby, but also giving small amounts of water or water-based drinks such as tea.

Full breastfeeding: Full breastfeeding means either exclusively or predominantly.

Bottle feeding: Bottle feeding means feeding a baby from a bottle, whatever is in the bottle, including expressed breast milk.

Artificial feeding: Artificial feeding means feeding a baby on artificial feeds, and not breastfeeding at all.

Partial breastfeeding: Partial breastfeeding means giving a baby some breast feeds, and some artificial feeds, either milk or cereal, or other food.

Timely complementary feeding: Timely complementary feeding means giving a baby other food in addition to breastfeeding, when it is appropriate, after the age of 4-6 months.

Breast conditions: There are several common breast conditions which many times cause difficulties with breastfeeding, i.e. flat or inverted nipples or long nipples or big nipples, engorgement, blocked duct acid mastitis, sore nipples and nipples fissure. There are many different shapes and sizes of breasts (Fig. 1.6). Babies can be breastfed from almost all of

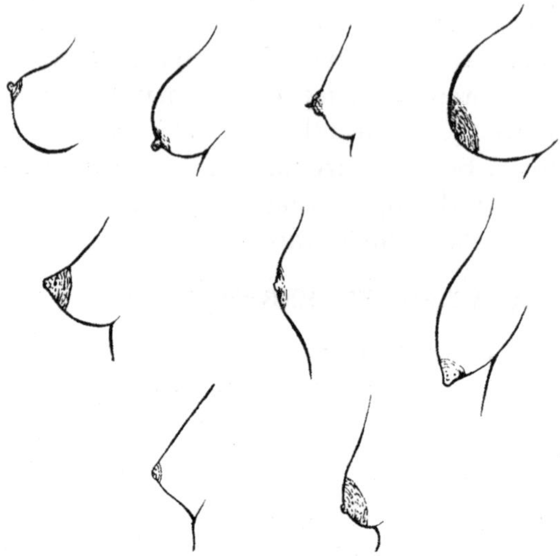

Fig. 1.6. There are many different shapes and sizes of breasts. Babies can breastfeed from almost all of them.

them (few common shapes and sizes of breast are shown in the figure above).

TEN STEPS TO SUCCESSFUL BREASTFEEDING

1. Train expectant mother in skills necessary to implement breastfeeding before child birth.
2. Inform pregnant woman about the benefits and management of breastfeeding.
3. Help mother initiate breastfeeding within half an hour of birth.
4. Show expectant mother how to breastfeed and how to maintain lactation.
5. Give new born infants no food or drink other than breast milk, unless medically indicated.
6. Practise rooming-in—allow mother and infant to remain together 24 hours.
7. Encourage breastfeeding on demand.
8. Give no artificial teats or pacifiers (also called dummies or soothers) to breastfeeding infants.

9. Ante-natal preparation for breastfeeding is a must. Explain benefits of breastfeeding, give simple relevant information on how to breastfeed. Explain her what happens after delivery.
10. Ask the expectant mother if she has any questions or worries. Examine her breasts if she is worried about them. Build her confidence.

WAYS TO BREASTFEED WHEN IN SITTING POSTURE

1. Put baby to your breast in the usual way. Observe the breastfeed.
2. Remember, the mother needs help to improve her baby's attachment. Breastfeeding might be more comfortable if baby takes larger mouthful of breast when he or she suckles (Fig. 1.7 and 1.8).
3. Make sure that you are sitting in a comfortable, relaxed position (Fig. 1.9). Sit down so that you are

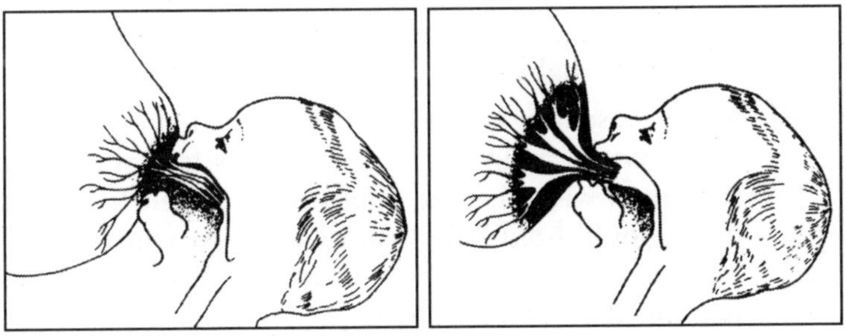

Fig. 1.7. Good and poor attachment (internal appearance)

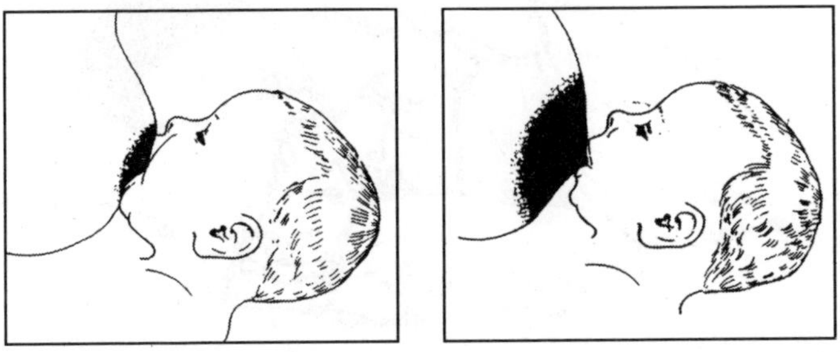

Fig. 1.8. Good and poor attachment (external appearance)

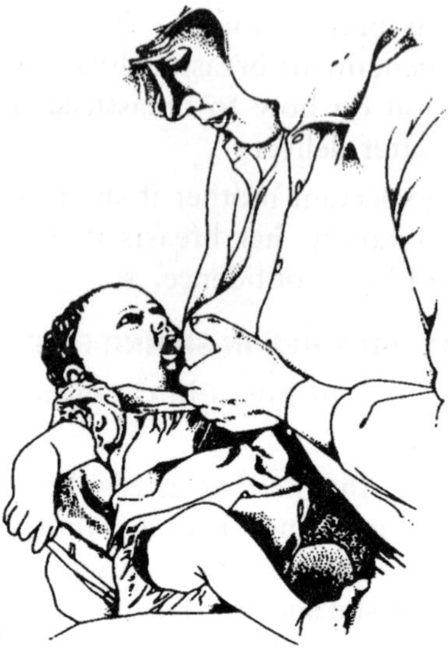

Fig. 1.9. Position of breastfeeding while sitting

comfortable and relaxed, and in a convenient position to feed the baby.

4. Make these four key points clear—the baby's head and body should be in a straight line, his face should face the breast with his nose opposite the nipple (Fig. 1.10). You should hold baby's body close to you and if the baby is newborn, support his or her bottom, and not just his head and shoulders.

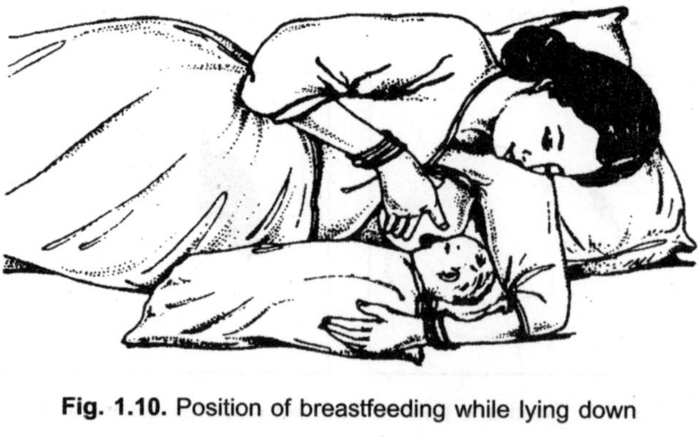

Fig. 1.10. Position of breastfeeding while lying down

5. Now support your breast with your hand to offer it to the baby. Rest fingers on chest wall under the breast, so that first finger forms a support at the base of the breast. Now use your thumb to press the top of breast slightly. This can improve the shape of the breast so that it is easier for baby to attach well. Do not hold breast too near to the nipple (Fig. 1.11).

Fig. 1.11. Holding the baby in arms while feeding

6. Touch baby's lips with your nipple, so that he or she opens mouth.
7. Wait until your baby's mouth is opening wide, before you move him onto your breast. Your baby's mouth needs to be wide open to take a large mouthful of breast.
8. Now quickly move the baby to your breast, when the baby is opening mouth wide, bring baby to your breast. You should not move yourself or your breast to the baby.
9. Bring your baby's lower lip below the nipple, so that chin touches your breast. Ensure you do not seem to have pain when your baby is suckling (Fig. 1.12).

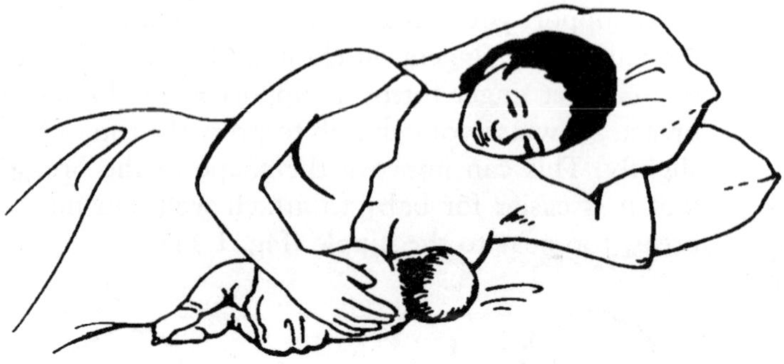

Fig. 1.12. A mother breastfeeding her baby lying down

Look for all the signs of good attachment. If the attachment is not good, try again. Lie down in a comfortable, relaxed position. It is better not to lie propped up on elbows, as this can make it difficult for the baby to attach to the breast.

2

Definitions of Terms for Breastfeeding and Health

Abscess of breast: Presence of painful, red swelling on the breast. The presence of pus caused due to infection.

After-pains: Contraction of the uterus during breastfeeding few days after childbirth, due to oxytocin released.

Alveoli: Sacs of milk-secreting cells in the breast.

Amenorrhoea: Absence of menstruation.

Anaemia: Lack of the red cells or haemoglobin in the blood.

Antenatal preparation: Preparing a mother for the delivery.

Antibodies: Proteins in the blood and breast milk to fight infection.

Areola: Dark skin surrounding the nipple.

Artificial feeds: Milk or other liquid given instead of breastfeeding.

Artificially fed: Receiving artificial feeds and no breast milk.

Attachment: The way a baby takes the breast into mouth; a baby may be well-attached or poorly-attached to the breast.

Bedding-in: A baby sleeping in bed with mother, instead of in a separate cot.

Blocked duct: A milk duct in the breast becoming blocked with thickened milk, so that the milk in that part of the breast does not flow out.

Bonding: Mother and baby developing a close loving relationship.

Breast pump: Device for expressing milk.

Breast refusal: A baby not wanting to suckle from his mother's breast.

Breastfeeding history: All the relevant information about a mother and baby and their present breastfeeding situation developed.

Breastfeeding supplementer: A tube through which a baby drinks artificial milk or expressed breast milk while suckling.

Breastfeeding support: Mothers who help each other to breastfeed.

Breast shells: Also known as breast shield and are used when nipples are flat.

Breast milk substitutes: Food or drink used to replace breast milk and breastfeeding.

Calories: Kilocalories to measure the energy available in food.

Candida: Yeast which can infect the nipple, baby's mouth and bottom, causing thrush.

Casein: Protein in milk which forms curds.

Cleft lip or palate: Abnormal division of the lip or palate.

Colic: Regular crying, sometimes with signs suggesting abdominal pain by the baby.

Cold compress: A piece of cloth soaked in cold water to put on the breast.

Colostrum: The special breast milk that women produce in few days after delivery; it is yellowish or clear in colour.

Complementary foods: Solid foods given from the age of 4-6 months.

Contaminated: Containing harmful bacteria or substances.

Dehydration: Lack of water in the body.

Demand feeding: Feeding a baby whenever he or she is ready. This is also called 'unrestricted' or 'baby-led' feeding.

Distraction: A baby's attention taken from the breast, e.g. noise.

Ducts: Tubes which lead milk to the nipple.

Dummy: Artificial nipple for a baby to suck, a pacifier.

Early contact: A mother holding her baby during the first hour or two after delivery.

Eczema: Skin condition associated with allergy.

Effective suckling: Suckling in a way which removes the milk efficiently from the breast.

Empathize: Show that you understand how a person feels from her point of view.

Engorgement: Swollen with breast milk, blood and tissue fluid. Engorged breasts are often painful, the milk does not flow well.

Essential fatty acids: Fats which are essential for a baby's growing eyes and brain, which are not present in cow's milk.

Exclusively breastfed: Breastfed only, with no other food, drink or water.

Eructation: The curdled milk baby brings out after feed.

Express: To squeeze or press out milk.

Expressed breast milk: Milk which is pressed out of the breasts.

Fissure: Break or a crack in the skin.

Flat nipple: A nipple which sticks out less than average.

Foremilk: Watery breast milk produced early in a feed.

Formula: Artificial milk for babies made out of a variety of products, including sugar, animal milk, soyabean and vegetable oils. They are usually in powder form, to mix with water.

Full breasts: Breasts which are full of milk, and hot, heavy and hard from which the milk flows.

Gastric suction: Sucking out a baby's stomach immediately after delivery.

Gestational age: The period baby completed in the uterus.

Growth factors: Substances in breast milk which promote growth and development of the intestine which help the intestine to recover after an attack of diarrhoea.

Growth spurt: Sudden increased hunger.

High needs babies: Babies who seem to need to be carried and comforted more than other babies.

Hindmilk: The fat-rich breast milk produced in a feed.

Hormones: Chemical messengers in the body.

Immune system: Those parts of the body and blood, including lymph glands and white blood cells, which fight infection.

Ineffective suckling: Suckling which removes milk from the breast inefficiently.

Infective mastitis: Mastitis due to bacterial infection.

Inverted nipple: A nipple which goes in instead of sticking out, or which goes in when the mother tries to stretch it out.

Inflammation: Skin becomes red and swollen.

Lactation: Process of producing breast milk.

Lactating: The period during which a woman is breastfeeding the baby.

Lactiferous sinuses: Ducts in which breast milk collects.

Lactose: The sugar present in milk.

Lumps in breast: A localized swelling in breast, painful to touch.

Low-birth-weight: Weighing less than 2.5 kg at birth.

Mastitis: Inflammation of the breast.

Mature milk: Breast milk produced after a few days.

Milk ejection reflex: Milk flowing from the breast due to oxytocin release when the baby suckles.

Milk stasis: Milk not flowing out of the breasts.

Montgomery's glands: Small glands in the areola which secrete an oily liquid.

"Nipple confusion": A term sometimes used to describe the way babies who are fed from a bottle may find it difficult to suckle effectively from a breast.

Nipple sucking: When a baby takes only the nipple into his mouth.

Non-infective mastitis: Mastitis due to milk leaking out of the alveoli and back into the breast tissues.

"Not enough milk": The common complaint of mothers who do not have enough breast milk for their babies.

Nutrients: Components of food.

Oedema: Swelling due to fluid in the tissue.

Oversupply: Too much milk produced by the breasts, sometimes flowing from the breast faster than the baby can take it.

Oxytocin: The hormone which makes the milk flow from the breast.

Pacifier: Artificial nipple made of plastic for a baby to suck.

Palpation: Examining by feeling with your hand.

Partially breastfed: Breastfeed given with some artificial feeds.

Placenta: A tissue which grows inside the uterus during pregnancy and links the body to the mother and helps growth and development of baby.

Predominantly breastfeed: Breastfeed is the main source of nourishment, but also given small amounts of non-nutritious drinks such as tea, water and water-based drinks.

Prelacteal feeds: Artificial feeds given before breastfeeding.

Prolactin: The hormone which makes the breasts produce milk.

Protein: Nutrient necessary for growth and repair of the body tissues.

Protractile: The nipple and underlying tissue needs to be stretched out for a baby to suckle effectively.

Rejection of baby: The mother not wanting to care her baby.

Relactation: A mother starting to breastfeed again and producing breast milk after she had stopped.

Restricted breastfeeds: When the frequency of breastfeed is limited.

Retained placenta: A small piece of the placenta remaining in the uterus after delivery.

Rooming-in: A baby staying in the same room with his mother.

Rooting: A baby searching for the breast with mouth.

Rooting reflex: A baby opening his mouth to find the nipple.

Rubber teat: The part of a feeding bottle from which a baby sucks.

Scissors hold: Holding the breast between the index and middle fingers while the baby is feeding.

Secrete: Produce a fluid in the body.

Self-weaning: A baby more than one year old deciding by himself to stop breastfeeding.

Sensory impulses: Message in nerves responsible for feeling.

Skin-to-skin contact: When a mother puts the baby on the breast.

Whey: Liquid part of milk which remains after removal of curds.

3

Tips for Breast Care during Pregnancy and Lactation

Pregnancy refers to the period beginning from the moment the woman conceives till she gives birth to the child. Lactation refers to the period during which a woman is breastfeeding her baby (Fig. 3.1). One of the most important sex organs in the female is the mamma (mammary gland), one on each side of the breast, jutting out as rounded firm masses, almost spherical in shape in a mature young virgin. In the centre there is a pink areola, with a small projection called lie nipple. On the surface

Fig. 3.1. Breastfeeding

of the nipple, there are 8 to 10 small openings of the milk duct. Mamma appears at the age of about 11 to 12 in a girl and gradually keeps on enlarging due to the increasing amount of blood supplied by nature. It is then tender to touch and feels warmer. On pressure a slight watery, colorless secretion can be squeezed out of it. After the birth of the baby, on the third day, these glands become very tense and milk begins to pour out. The pink colour of the areola takes on a darker tinge. The nipples become prominent and projecting during pregnancy and particularly after suction by the baby.

The mamma is made of glandular tissues which are collected as small lobules (Fig. 3.2). They are lined first by cubical cells which secrete milk. The lobules are held together by fibrous tissue and fat to give it the rounded appearance. Out of these small lobules, the milk comes out through a small narrow passage called a duct, and many such ducts or tributaries unite to form 8 to 10 main ducts which open on the nipple. Psychological and manual irritation (titillation of the nipples and pressing the bulbs) hardens the mamma and stimulates the

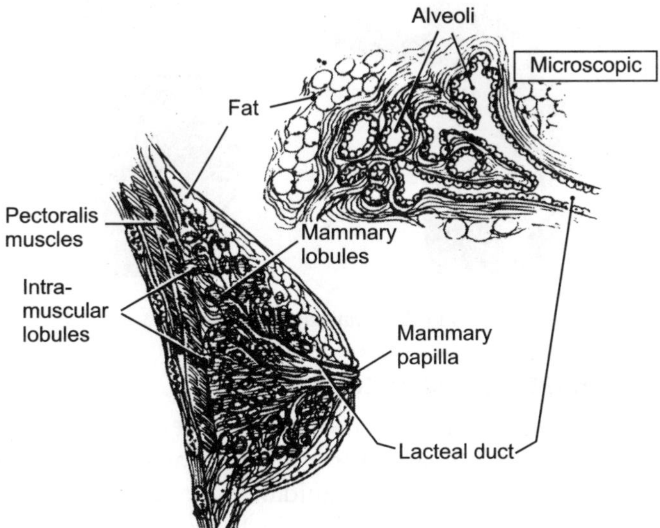

Fig. 3.2. Structure of breast

sexual urge in the female more easily when they are in a firm condition. Firm and elastic bulbs are indeed every woman's pride and privilege and can be maintained by proper treatment and precautions. The important precaution for maintaining shapely breasts is the use of proper brassieres which give necessary ease and comfort to the breasts. But for every defect in the development of breasts, it is always necessary to consult a specialist for some timely treatment. Normally, after pregnancy and delivery, there is a danger of the breasts becoming loose and drooping. There are certain medicines and massage oils, which help the breasts to come to their normal form and shape and regain firmness and roundness (Fig. 3.3). Physical breast care is very important. Active and regular participation in sports helps a woman to maintain a distinctive and smart look. Thus, youthful breasts not only add to the grace of the woman but also enrich her sex life as well.

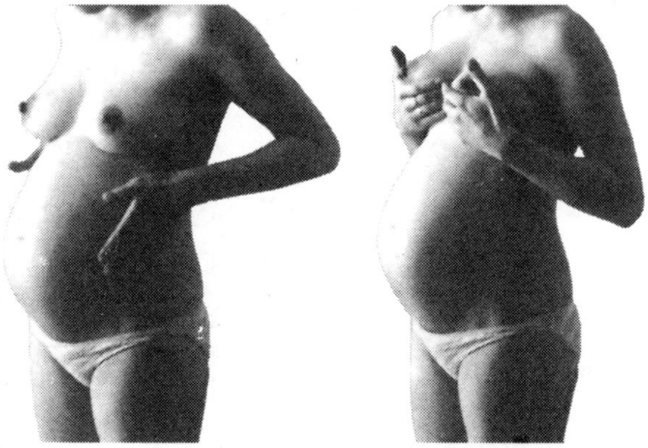

Fig. 3.3. Massaging breasts

BREASTS CARE DURING PREGNANCY

In order to breastfeed the baby successfully, a pregnant woman should be prepared for it mentally as well as physically. It is also useful to seek the guidance of a woman who has successfully breastfed her baby. Such women can give good practical advice.

It is also advised that a woman should share her thoughts on this topic with her husband, or with any other woman close to her. During pregnancy, eat more than the normal diet, roughly eat equal to one extra meal in a day. This will help build enough energy, to be used when you start breastfeeding your baby (Fig. 3.4). Pregnant woman should eat foods which are rich in iron and assist in producing more blood. This will help to prevent anaemia. Do not tire yourself physically (especially during the last three months) when you are pregnant. A nap or rest in the afternoon is essential during the last three months.

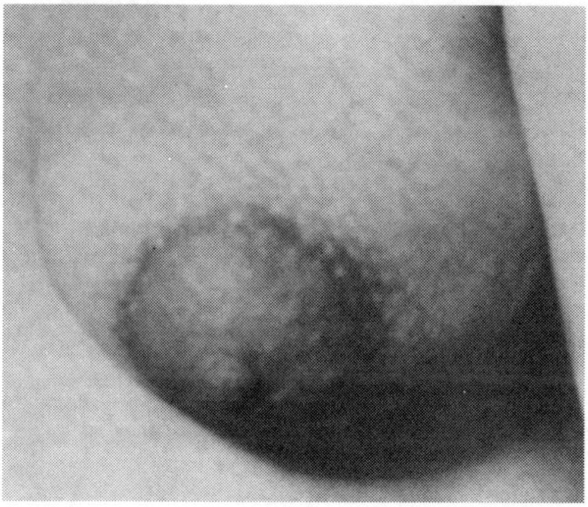

Fig. 3.4. Changes in breast associated with pregnancy

CLOTHING TO WEAR DURING PREGNANCY

The figure and shape of the breasts (Fig. 3.5) greatly depend on the clothes you wear during pregnancy and lactation, so make a careful choice of clothes. The bra should be made of cotton and not of synthetic material. It should be well-fitting to be able to support the extra weight of the breasts during pregnancy and lactation. At the same time, the bra should not be so tight as to squash or compress the breasts. Pressure on the breasts can produce a collapse of milk production glands besides causing pain and irritation. The bra should open at the front, either with a clip or laces, so that it is easy to fasten and undo (Fig. 3.6). After childbirth, it is necessary to know what to wear.

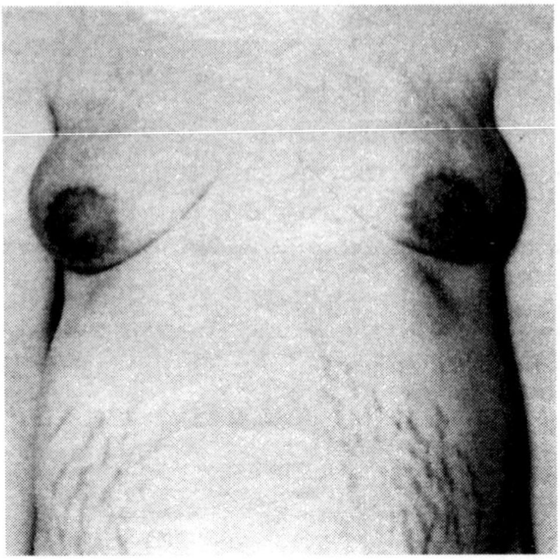

Fig. 3.5. Striae gravidarum on the breast as a result of stretching by fatty deposits

Fig. 3.6. Clothing during pregnancy

Do not try to expose the breasts to feed your child by pulling the bra up or down. Some women do not prefer to wear a bra during the period of pregnancy or lactation. It is alright during pregnancy, if the breasts are small and a support is not required. However, during the lactation period, when the breasts are usually heavy, one must use a bra. During the night, the bra may be removed. Some absorbent material may be required at night to prevent the sheets from getting soiled due to any leakage of breast milk.

During the day time, several brassieres are required during the lactation period, as they are likely to be soiled often by leakage of milk. To avoid this problem, it is wise to keep a cotton cloth or a piece of clean diaper to soak the leakage. Do not put tissue or cotton wool, these can stick to the nipples and create problems when removing them. During the summer season, avoid nylon or silk brassieres, these may cause rashes and allergic reactions on the delicate skin of the breasts.

Wearing a brassiere is necessary during pregnancy: Breasts become very heavy during pregnancy because of the hormones secreted in preparation of feeding the baby. Do not get worried about this change. Support the breasts with the appropriate size of bras capable of allowing the enlargement of breasts as during the period of pregnancy, breasts tend to grow faster. It would be useful to handle the breasts during pregnancy, so that there is no difficulty when handling them at the time of breastfeeding. Take care to prevent your breasts from being compressed during sleep so they do not hurt. Remember, the breasts should be kept clean.

CARING OF THE NIPPLES

One in every twenty women usually suffers from a disorder of the nipple. Remember that a poor nipple shape which would interfere with feeding is uncommon. There is no need to worry if nipples stick out. In case the nipples appear flat or inverted (Fig. 3.7), then it is advised to press the areola between the thumb and the finger to encourage the nipple to stand out. If the nipple sticks out, the baby will not have any difficulty in suckling.

During the pregnancy period the shape of the nipple may be abnormal, but it improves as the pregnancy advances. This is

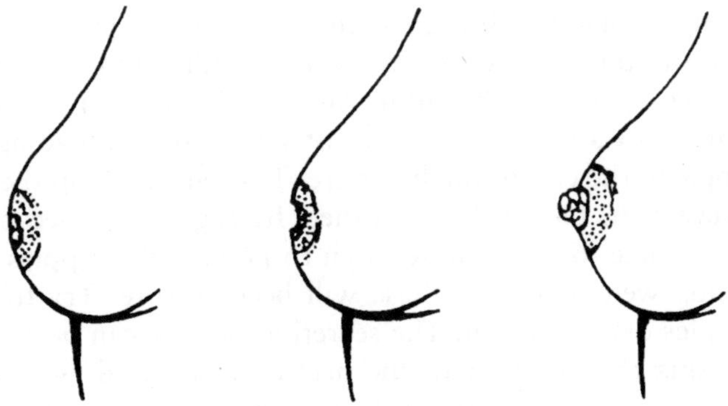

Fig. 3.7. Caring of nipples

because of the effect of hormones during pregnancy. Do not apply any ointment or a cream to the nipples. Do not apply soap to the nipples. Clean the nipples by splashing water on them. Do not try to remove any secretions, since these are protective and prevent infection.

OILY DISCHARGE FROM THE NIPPLES

Sometimes, there is an oily discharge from the nipples during pregnancy and after childbirth for a few days, young women get worried on seeing the oozing liquid. Around the areola of the breasts, there are small glands (called Montgomery's Tubercles) which secrete small amount of a greasy material which kills the germs on the skin in this area. The greasy material is also useful in keeping the nipples supple. Do not wash nipples with soap to clean the greasy material, otherwise there will be a possibility that the nipples might become sore when the baby suckles them. All that needs to be done is to splash the nipples with plain water to keep them clean. Suckling of breasts during pregnancy is not harmful. If the husband wishes to suck the breasts, he should not be discouraged. This is a natural and helpful exercise for the nipples and the breasts.

LEAKING OF MILK FROM BREASTS

Oozing of milk from the breast during the last stage of pregnancy in the ninth month and the first few weeks after the baby is born is common. This indicates that the breast is full and the mother is ready to breastfeed the baby (Fig. 3.8). The sight, sound and thought of breastfeeding sometimes cause a thrilling sensation in the breasts and secretion of milk from the nipples. Do not worry, it's not harmful. All you need to do is to keep a soft napkin or a hanky or a piece of soft cloth or a pad against the nipple in the cup of the brassiere. This will soak up the milk and prevent the blouse, bra and sheet from getting soiled. Make sure to change this pad quite often to prevent the nipples from remaining wet, otherwise these will become sore. Try to keep the nipples dry and clean. The secretion of milk can be stopped by pressing the nipple with the heel of your hand against the breast for about one minute. In case the milk drips from the

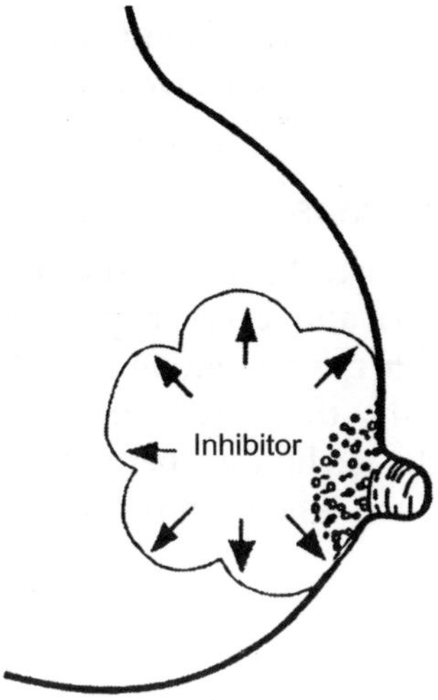

Fig. 3.8. Inhibitor in breast milk

other breast while feeding the baby, just leave the breast exposed and let the milk drip on a hanky or a clean diaper.

IS LACTATION A SAFE PERIOD?

Many women think that the period of breastfeeding (Lactation period) is also a safe period and they continue to feed the baby for two or three years under the impression that by doing so, they will be safe from conceiving during this period. They believe that during the period of breastfeeding, menstruation will not take place and so conception cannot take place. But it is absolutely untrue that suckling in itself is a safe method of contraception. Normally, after 9 or 10 months of the delivery, a woman begins to menstruate. In many cases menstruation may begin even as early as in the second or third month. It is suggested that when the baby is 7 or 8 months old, it should be weaned away, otherwise it will adversely affect the health of both the mother and the child. A woman who becomes pregnant again while feeding one baby will harm not only herself and the baby but also the expectant child in her womb. I know many such women who are under the impression that conception will not take place during the lactation period. They did not menstruate, but on examination, it was found that they were pregnant. To sum up, this method has proved unreliable and undependable.

EXPRESSION OF MILK FROM BREASTS

Expression of milk from the breasts means squeezing out the milk from the breast (Fig. 3.9) and every expectant woman should be fully conversant with the technique and the correct procedure. It is also important that they should have full knowledge and practice of the technique beforehand as this would prevent panic and failure when expression is actually required.

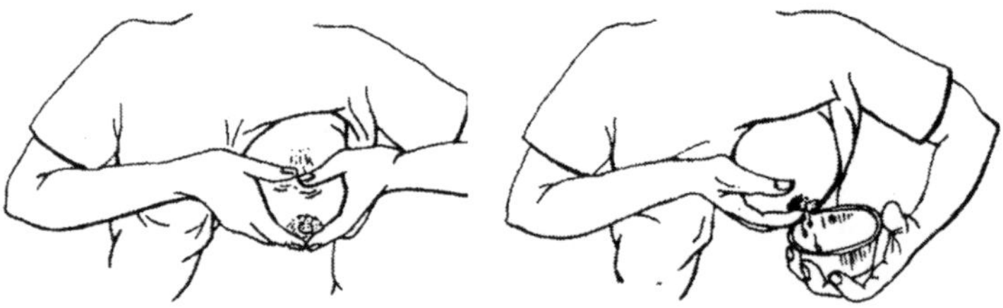

Fig. 3.9. Expressing milk

Breast milk may have to be expressed: (i) If the baby is very weak and premature, and therefore, cannot suckle. (ii) Mother is sick and hospitalized or the baby is sick. (iii) If the nipple is sore or the breasts are engorged, resulting breastfeeding very painful and (iv) If the mother has to go out and is unable to take the baby along with her.

Procedure for Expressing Breast Milk

- Wash and clean the hands before starting expression of breast milk. Milk should be collected in a clean bottle or clean container with a cover.
- Express the breast with one hand and use the other hand for collecting the milk. Hold the breast in the hand and hold the areola between the thumb and the first finger.
- Now gently squeeze the areola with your hand, press the breast towards the chest. After repeating this two

to three times, the milk will begin to squirt out intermittently.

- Keep squeezing the areola in between the spurts to encourage the hind-milk. Both hands can be used and the help of someone else may be taken to collect the milk.
- During the expression of milk, the milk comes out slowly in comparison to natural suckling. The procedure helps to empty the breasts as well as to stimulate them to keep producing the milk.
- Do not freeze or boil the expressed milk, as this will reduce its nutritious value and affect its useful properties.

A breast pump may be used to express the milk. Breast pumps are readily available in the market. Guidance for the operation of the breast pump can be obtained from the lady doctor.

SHAPE OF BREAST DUE TO FEEDING

However, breasts do change the shape as a result of breastfeeding. The nipples of the breast also enlarge and darken during pregnancy. They never lose their pigment subsequently because milk is secreted and stored in the breast. They may enlarge further during lactation. Care should be taken to preserve the shape of breasts. Use of well-fitting bras support the breasts and help in retaining their shape. With proper care, a lot can be done to restore their lost shape. A better understanding and a harmonious relationship can do a lot for a woman to remain as attractive and acceptable to a man after breastfeeding the baby as without it.

BREAST CONTOURING

Breasts have their own muscles. They consist mainly of mammary glands and fat. The breasts are held in position by the skin and by the fibrous tissue which connect the bosom to the pectoral muscles. Strangely enough, exercises are similar whether you want to increase or decrease the size of the bust. The only difference is that if your bust measurement is too large, you should do the exercises fairly rapidly and do breast massage. The main causes are:

Overdevelopment in puberty: Female hormones cause breasts to grow rapidly during puberty. Sometimes the breasts may grow to a pathologically abnormally large size.

Pregnancy overdevelopment: During pregnancy, for three to four months, the breasts become enlarged and after the delivery, with the skin stretching, the breasts sag even though they may regain their former size.

Overdevelopment due to obesity: Usually women suffering from obesity have overdeveloped breasts (Fig. 3.10). This is known as "Fatty Macromastia". The gland-fat relationship is

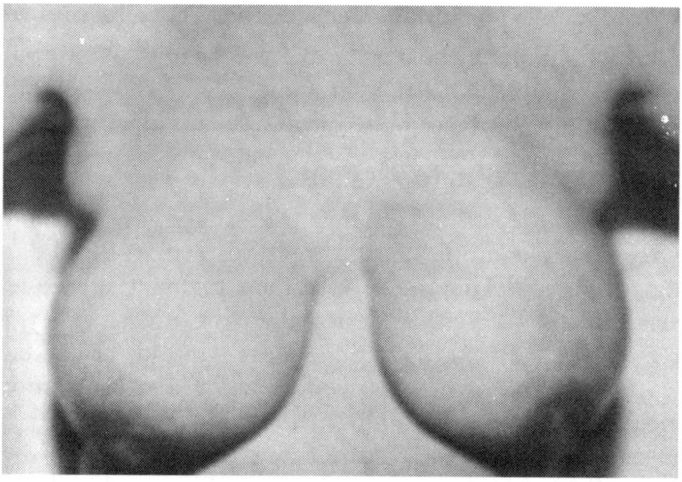

Fig. 3.10. Overdeveloping breasts – the active breast tissue extending into the axilla

altered during menopause, and fat largely replaces the glands, leading to a change in size and shape of breasts after maternity (Fig. 3.11). Largeness of breasts depends on the size of the patient.

Symptoms: The abnormal, enlarged breast women feel the following symptoms:

1. The weight of the breasts puts a strain upon the cervical and thoracic spine, producing neck pain and backache.

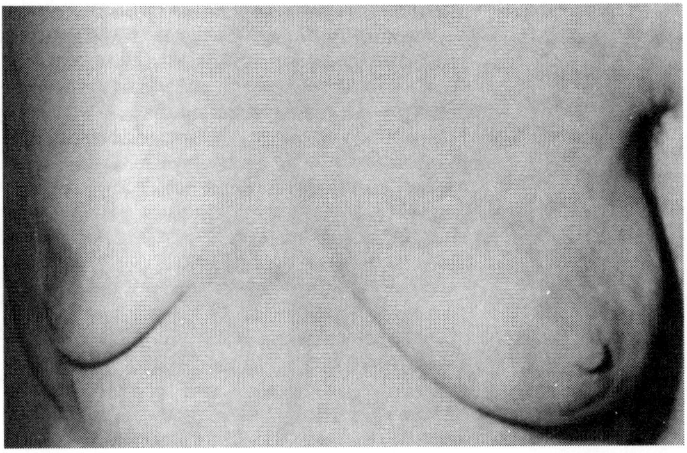

Fig. 3.11. A woman with left breast larger than right

2. The brassiere may seem a painful embodiment during the menstrual period.
3. Sagging of the breasts also creates problems between the lower part of the breasts and the chest wall.
4. Fitting of clothes needs extensive alterations.
5. Breast over-enlargement prevents movements and hard work.
6. It destroys the glamour of the body.
7. Due to heavy breast weight, there is always a pressure of the bra on the neck or nerve plexus.

WHAT IS COLOSTRUM?

Colostrum is a liquid slightly yellow in colour and thick in consistency. It is secreted from the breasts during the first few days after the delivery of a child. In the olden days, the colostrum was thrown away believing that it was unfit for the child, being the accumulated milk of pregnancy. Some called it pus and thought it was harmful for the child. The truth is colostrum is not harmful for newborn babies. In fact, it must be given to a newborn baby as it is rich in proteins, minerals and vitamins (Fig. 3.12). It is low in fat and carbohydrates. Colostrum

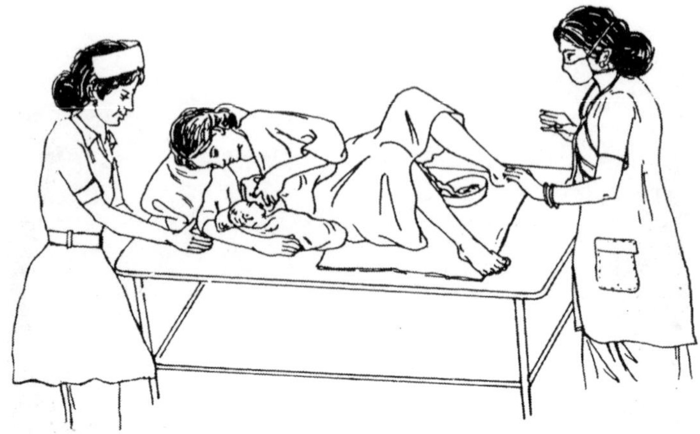

Fig. 3.12. A mother breastfeeding her newborn baby soon after delivery

provides the child with a lot of antibodies and protects the child against infections and allergies in later life.

BREASTFEEDING LEADS TO CANCER

There is wrong conception that breastfeeding leads to breast cancer in later life. This is untrue. Rather, women who do not breastfeed their babies or remain unmarried have a greater chance of developing breast cancer in later life. Every young expectant woman is advised to seek the advice of a lady doctor for correct guidance. Difficulties arise due to lack of confidence or experience. Do not get discouraged, if you do not succeed in the first few attempts or if it takes a long time for the milk to come out.

Initially, after childbirth, sometimes a very small amount of milk is produced in the beginning. In such cases, artificial milk is given to the baby to make up for the milk deficiency. This may prove harmful. Remember: The artificial feed may be unhygienically prepared and may cause infection in the new-born child. It has no substantial food value and delays the administration of breast milk. The artificial milk may occasionally choke the baby if not given in the correct way.

Moreover, breast milk provided by nature is secreted by the mother in accordance with the child's requirement, which is small during the first few days after birth and gradually increases. Usually, a newborn baby is handed over to the mother soon after the birth. The mother should hold the baby and put him to breast. At this time, the body releases certain hormones helping the placenta, which grows inside the uterus during pregnancy and links the baby to the mother. Blood is passed from the mother to the baby through the placenta. It helps in the growth and development of the baby. The hormones released during suckling help the womb to contract, thus reducing the bleeding. They also make the secretion and flow of milk easy. It is suggested that the first breastfeed must be given within half an hour of childbirth. During this period, the child is very eager to suckle.

BREASTFEEDING THE BABY WHO HAS JAUNDICE

Jaundice among breastfed babies is common and obvious when yellowness in the skin develops. This is generally because of breastfeeding, and because of the effect of the hormone in the breast milk. This jaundice does not harm the baby in any way. However, newborn babies may develop jaundice due to some other reason and occasionally this may be very harmful. Therefore, consult your doctor if signs of jaundice are visible on the baby's body (e.g. chest or abdomen) or on the palms of the hands or soles of the feet. At times, the jaundice in a breastfed baby may lead to stoppage of breastfeeding for a couple of days. You should not panic if the jaundice in breastfed babies sometimes lasts for more than a month, if this is not pronounced or severe.

SHOULD A VERY WEAK WOMAN BREASTFEED HER BABY?

Weak, undernourished and even starving mothers produce breast milk and can successfully breastfeed their babies. However, such a mother will produce less milk than a well nourished mother. Though these women all over the world succeed in breastfeeding, they do this at the expense of their own health and nutrition. In the process of breastfeeding they may become even more undernourished and weak. It is, therefore, advised that such mothers should increase their diet. It is wiser to feed the lactating mother, rather than spending on powder milk or costly feeds for the baby.

SHOULD A CAESAREAN MOTHER BREASTFEED?

She can breastfeed her baby very successfully, though this may be slightly more difficult after a normal delivery. Put the baby to the breast as soon as it is possible after the mother regains consciousness. If she was given general anesthesia, then it might take a while for the effect of the sedatives and the anesthesia to wear off. In case she was given an epidural anesthesia, that is, the operation was done after an injection was administered, the delay will be minimal. Somebody will have to assist a Caesarean woman in positioning the baby for the feed. It is advised that the baby should be fed while the mother is lying down. Once the feeding has been completed on one side, roll over to the other side and ask the person helping you to move the baby to the other side, it will be harder to feed the baby while sitting up.

SHOULD A SICK CHILD BE BREASTFED?

There is no need to discontinue breastfeeding a sick baby due to several reasons. Breast milk supports the nutrition of the child during illness. It has been observed that breastfeeding helps the child to recover from an illness. It also prevents the occurrence of malnutrition which can be caused by illness and poor intake of nutritive food. Breast milk is particularly useful if the baby is suffering from diarrhoea. Breastfeeding provides emotional support which the baby requires during illness. It provides warmth to the baby because of the closeness to the mother's body and this may be life-saving in an infant below the age of eight weeks. On the other hand, a mother should continue breastfeeding, since this will help her to maintain her own milk supply.

SHOULD A SICK WOMAN BREASTFEED HER CHILD?

Breastfeeding should not be discontinued even when the mother is sick. Most of the time, the illness is not very severe and does not interfere with breastfeeding. In case, the mother had been hospitalized and the baby is not permitted to remain with the mother, the mother should express her milk and give it to the baby. It is possible that the medicine, the mother is given comes in large amounts in the breast milk. Find out from the doctor if the mother should temporarily discontinue feeding because of the risk from the medicine that she is taking. The mother may discontinue to breastfeed the baby if she feels too exhausted and uncomfortable to do so. Some women question whether women with AIDS/HIV should breastfeed their babies. The chances of passing on HIV/AIDS through breast milk are much less than through pregnancy and childbirth. A doctor should be consulted for this. If the woman has AIDS and is suffering from the symptoms of the disease, then it should be left to the woman to decide and if she feels strong enough, she may breastfeed the baby. Otherwise, artificial feeding should be considered.

SHOULD A WOMAN BREASTFEED WHEN SHE HAS BEEN GIVEN SEDATIVES?

During labour pains, sometimes sedatives are given to the expectant mother, as such the newly-delivered baby does not want to take the feeds. The common cause of the baby's lack of interest in breastfeeding is that since the woman has been given sleeping pills or sedatives during labour pains, the baby too comes under the effect of such sedatives. These medicines will have passed to the baby in the womb, so the baby is also sedated. In such cases, the effect of the sedatives remains for a few days and the baby will suckle the breast actively when the effect of the sedatives wears off. It is best to consult the doctor. However, to overcome this problem, the breast milk may be expressed and given to the baby with a spoon until the baby wakes up and starts suckling.

IN CASE OF TWINS, SHOULD I BREASTFEED BOTH?

Certainly, twins can be successfully breastfed. No need to worry or wonder whether the mother can produce enough milk for two babies. The quantity of milk a mother produces depends on the demand of the babies. If a mother wants to save time, she may feed both babies at the same time, but in this case she will have to find the most comfortable position to feed the twins. She must make sure that they do not drag the nipples while suckling, because this may make the nipples sore.

DIET FOR FEEDING MOTHERS

There are two problems related to feeding mothers. The first relates to the possible reduction in the supply of breast milk, if the mother's intake is little. The second relates to the mother becoming weak, if she doesn't eat enough during the lactation period. I do not agree that women who eat less or have an undernourished diet are not successful in breastfeeding. If a woman's intake of food is less, she will continue to produce milk by using her body's stores of food, but in this process she will become weak. The general rule is to eat according to the appetite. A feeding mother should not go on a dieting schedule and at the same time should not increase the intake of food inordinately. If a woman goes on a weight-reducing diet, she will become weak and malnourished. In case of an excess intake of diet, she will put on extra weight. Always eat what you have been eating before pregnancy. Many mothers believe that if they drink more milk, they will secrete more milk. This is a myth. Eat a balanced diet. A woman will however need extra calcium to supply to the baby. Bread, cabbage, cheese and milk are rich source of calcium. There is no need to take extra vitamins, if a mother is eating a balanced diet. Remember, what suits a mother will also suit her baby. Foods, if taken in excess, will disturb the digestive system of the mother and will also upset the baby. A feeding mother should avoid strong spices or condiments as this gives the baby a mild digestive upset. Sometimes (very rarely) egg or cow's milk taken by the mother may cause an allergy in the baby.

SMOKING AND DRINKING BY FEEDING MOTHERS

Better cut down or completely stop smoking while breastfeeding your baby. The nicotine from the cigarette passes into breast milk and this will make the baby restless, excited and unable to sleep. Remember, excessive smoking is known to reduce breast milk. Smoking can also cause lack of sleep in you, thereby reducing the flow of milk. Passive smoking may affect the baby. It is suggested that no one should smoke close to a baby or in the room where the baby is sleeping. The baby will inhale the smoke and may suffer from lung infection. The alcohol that you drink will get to your baby through your breast milk. Approximately, a ten per cent content of the liquor you consume will get into your breast milk and the baby will get a dose from the breast milk. Reports are available about the ill-effects suffered by those breastfed babies whose mothers have a light intake of alcohol. However, a minute quantity of alcohol will not harm you or your baby. However, drinking tea or coffee is not harmful to mother or baby. They do not affect the breast milk supply. But do not drink tea or coffee in excess. An excess of anything is harmful.

ARE MEDICINES HARMFUL?

As far as possible, lactating mothers should avoid taking medicines, since these will be passed on to the baby in some amounts through breast milk. Medicines sometimes affect the milk supply. Even a small amount of some medicines may harm the baby. There are some medicines which may produce an allergy in the baby. It is better to avoid use of medicines as far as possible if you are breastfeeding your child. Tell your doctor clearly that you are a breastfeeding mother, so that he can take this into account while prescribing medicines to you. It may be possible for the doctor to replace a medicine that is possibly harmful for the baby. There may be some medicines which may have to be taken even though they may be harmful for the baby. Breast milk should not be given to the baby as long as any potentially harmful medicine is being given to the mother. During this time, the baby may be given artificial milk with a spoon. The mother should express her milk as frequently as possible and throw it away during the period she is taking the medicine. Expressing of breast milk is very essential, as this will help to maintain her milk supply. Remember, antibiotics like chloramphenicol, cotrimoxazole, sulfa drugs, tetracycline, penicillin, metronidazole, nalidixic acid, nitrofurantoin and novobiocin should be avoided by lactating mothers.

PRECAUTION REGARDING SEX

Breastfeeding should not interfere with sex or sexual relationships as long as you as well as your husband's attitude is positive. It is also known that mothers who breastfeed their babies return to their normal physical fitness and body anatomy faster than mothers who feed their babies on artificial milk. This is because of the hormones produced by the lactating mother. It is also known that mothers who breastfeed babies are likely to have a harmonious sexual relationship. During lactation there is nothing wrong in having intercourse with your husband. There is nothing wrong, if your husband fondles your breasts and even suckles them, if this is acceptable to both of you. If the breasts are painful or if the problem of leakage is there, it is better to have sex after breastfeeding the baby. If it is difficult to have sex in certain positions because of the pain in the breast, then look for a more comfortable position.

WHETHER BREASTFEEDING PROTECTS PREGNANCY

Though breastfeeding does have a protective contraceptive effect, one cannot totally depend on the protection. The hormones produced when breastfeeding may prevent pregnancy. But you should not depend fully on this protection. If you breastfeed your baby totally, then you can expect good protection initially for eight to ten weeks. However, I have seen a case in which a woman re-conceived six weeks after the baby was born. It has been observed that if a baby is kept fully on breastfeed and is breastfed a minimum of at least ten times a day, then the chances of pregnancy for about four months are rare. Remember it is not advisable to depend on the return of periods. A woman may even conceive without having started her period. In rural women and amongst tribals, the protection seems to be better than in urban educated women. This is because tribal and rural women practice natural and totally unrestricted breastfeeding. They are generally undernourished and there are taboos against sex during lactation. These factors are not relevant to the urban educated woman who breastfeeds her child. It is advised not to depend upon the contraceptive effect given by hormones totally.

Mothers who want hundred per cent protection against pregnancy are advised to use contraceptive method. Oral contraceptive pills are not advised as a method of contraception during breastfeeding. Oral pills may contain certain hormones which reduce the supply of breast milk. These pills also affect the quality of breast milk, since the hormones from the pills are passed on to the baby. The hormones in the pills may have several bad effects on the baby, such as causing jaundice, enlargement of baby's breasts and changes in the baby's genitalia and bones.

SHOULD A MOTHER BREASTFEED THE CHILD AFTER CONCEIVING AGAIN?

Generally, during the first few months of breastfeeding, pregnancy does not occur. If it does, you may continue breastfeeding without any problem. The quantity of milk secreted during pregnancy may decline but the quality will not be affected. However, if you continue breastfeeding, the quality of colostrum in the milk for the next baby will be affected. So it is advised that breastfeeding should be reduced gradually and stopped. Till such time as you do continue feeding the baby, you should increase the diet according to your appetite. You need to eat for the baby growing in your womb as well as to cover the needs of breastfeeding.

WHAT IS THE CORRECT TIME TO STOP BREASTFEEDING?

There is no hard and fast rule about when to stop breastfeeding and every woman should know that after the age of eight months, there are no medical benefits of breast milk to the child. After the age of one year, breast milk is simply a liquid food for the baby. There is no absolute age limit for breastfeeding, after the age of one year, it provides only psychological satisfaction, physical comfort and some food value. In rural and tribal area, women usually breastfeed their babies till they are two, three or even four years old. A woman has to decide for herself how long to continue breastfeeding her baby. In case, she feels embarrassed because of the comments of other people, she can feed the baby in private. Breastfeeding should not be discontinued before the baby is four to six months of age. Semi-solid food should never be given before the age of four months, and at the same time, it must not be delayed beyond the age of eight months. The process of discontinuing breastfeeding should be slow. This will prevent the baby from becoming fretful and the breast from becoming painful or tense. There are several medicines available in the market that dry up the milk. These medicines are not advised. Some old women advise rubbing the nipples and the areola with some substances which taste awful, to discourage the baby from wanting to be breastfed. These are also not advised. Some babies enjoy suckling the nipple and such babies should be offered a bottle when being given artificial milk. Remember, that the feeding bottle and the nipple should be clean. Discontinue the evening feed first. Then keep discontinuing the feeds one at a time after an interval of 4 or 5 days. The last feeds which should be dropped are the early morning and the late night feeds, since discontinuing these first might produce tension and pain in your breasts.

Breastfeed a baby during periods: Periods do not affect the quality and quantity of breast milk. However, pre-menstrual tension may affect the quantity to some extent.

4

Ten Commandments of Happy Breastfeeding

EXPRESSING BREAST MILK

There are many situations in which expressing breast milk is useful and important to enable a mother to initiate or continue breastfeeding. Expressing milk is useful to relieve engorgement, relieve blocked duct or milk stasis, feed a baby while he learns to suckle from an inverted nipple, feed a baby who has difficulty in co-ordinating suckling, feed a baby who refuses while he learns to enjoy breastfeeding, feed a low-birth-weight baby who cannot be breastfed, feed a sick baby who cannot suckle enough, keep up the supply of breast milk when a mother or baby is ill, leave breast milk for a baby when his mother goes out to work, prevent leaking when a mother is away from her baby, help a baby to attach to a full breast, express breast milk directly into a baby's mouth, prevent the nipple and areola from becoming dry and sore. It is a good idea for all mothers to learn how to express their breast milk and know what to do if the need arises.

The most useful way for a mother to express milk is by hand. It needs no appliance, so she can do it anywhere and at any time. With a good technique, it can be very efficient. It is easy to hand-express when the breasts are soft. It is more difficult when the breasts are engorged or tender. So learn how to hand-express on the first or second day after delivery. Many mothers are able to express plenty of breast milk using rather strange techniques. If a mother's technique works for her, let her do it that way. But if a mother is having difficulty in expressing enough milk, she must learn a more effective technique. The oxytocin reflex may not work as well when a mother expresses as it does when a baby suckles. A mother needs to know how to help her oxytocin reflex, or she may find it difficult to express her milk.

How to Express Breast Milk by Hand

- Wash your hands thoroughly.
- Sit or stand comfortably, and hold the container near your breast (Fig. 4.1(a)).

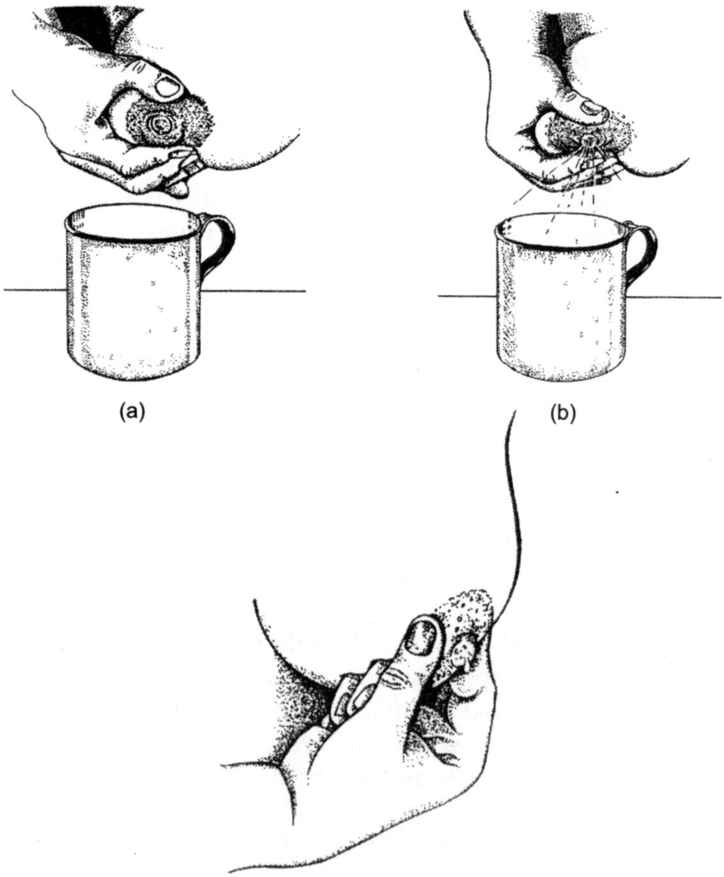

(a) (b) (c)

Fig. 4.1. Expressing milk with hand

- Put your thumb on the breast ABOVE the nipple and areola, and your first finger on the breast BELOW the nipple and areola, opposite the thumb. Support the breast with your other fingers (Fig. 4.1(b)).
- Press your thumb and first finger slightly inwards towards the chest wall. You should avoid pressing too far, that can block the milk ducts (Fig. 4.1(c)).
- Press your breast behind the nipple and areola between your finger and thumb. You must press on the lactiferous sinuses beneath the areola. Sometimes, in a lactating breast it is possible to feel the sinuses. They are like pods, or peanuts. If you can feel them, you can press on them.
- Press and release, press and release. This should not hurt; if it hurts, the technique is wrong. At first no milk may come, but after pressing a few times, milk starts to drip out. It may flow in streams if the oxytocin reflex is active (Fig. 4.2).

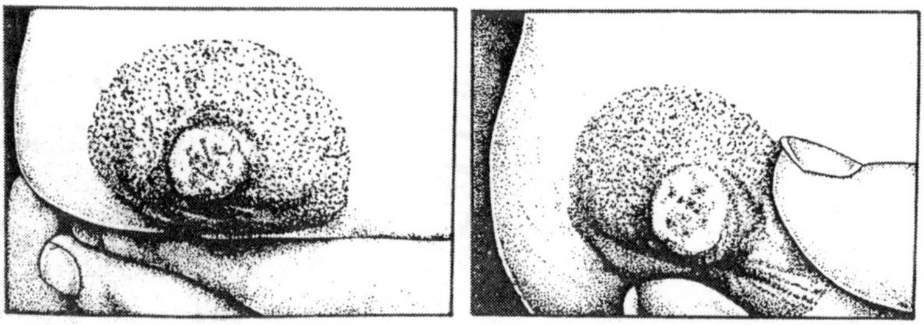

Fig. 4.2. Holding the breast when breastfeeding

- Press the areola in the same way from the sides, to make sure that milk is expressed from all segments of the breast.
- Avoid rubbing or sliding your fingers along the skin. The movement of the fingers should be more like rolling.
- Avoid squeezing the nipple itself. Pressing or pulling the nipple cannot express the milk. It is the same as the baby sucking only the nipple.

- Express one breast for at least 3-5 minutes until the flow slows; then express the other side and then repeat both sides. You can use either hand for either breast and change when they get tired.

How to Express Breast Milk

- Place finger and thumb on each side of the areola and press inwards towards the chest wall.
- Press behind the nipple and areola between your finger and thumb.
- Press from the sides to empty all segments.

Expressing Breast Milk with Breast Pump

If hand expression is difficult, a mother can use a hand-operated breast pump (Fig. 4.3). Rubber bulb pumps are not very efficient, especially when the breasts are soft. They are not suitable for collecting milk to feed a baby. They are difficult to clean properly. Milk may collect in the rubber bulb and it is

Fig. 4.3. A mother expressing her breast milk through hand-operated breast pump

difficult to clean out. The milk which collects is often contaminated. They are useful mainly to relieve engorgement or when hand expression is difficult. They are often called 'breast relievers'. Syringe pumps are more efficient than rubber bulb pumps. They are easier to clean and sterilize. To use a syringe pump, put the plunger inside the outer cylinder. Make sure that the rubber seal is in good flexible condition. Now put the funnel over the nipple, make sure that it touches the skin all around. To make an air- tight seal, pull the outer cylinder down. The nipple is sucked into the funnel. Release the outer cylinder, and then pull down again. After a minute or two, milk starts to flow and collects in the outer cylinder. When milk stops flowing, break the seal, pour out the milk and then repeat the procedure.

The warm bottle method for the expression of breast milk: This is a useful technique to relieve severe engorgement, when a breast is very tender, and the nipple is tight, so that hand expression is difficult. You need a suitable bottle made of glass, not plastic (1-3 litres in size but not smaller than 700 ml) with a wide neck (at least 2 to 4 cm diameter) that the nipple can fit into it easily. You also need a pan of hot water to warm the bottle, some cold water to cool the neck of the bottle and a thick cloth to hold the hot bottle. Pour a little of the hot water into the bottle to start warming it up. Then almost fill the bottle with hot water. Do not fill it right up too quickly or the glass will crack. Let the bottle stand for a few minutes to warm the glass. Wrap the bottle in the cloth and pour hot water back into the pan. Cool the neck of the bottle with cold water, inside and outside (If you do not cool the neck of the bottle, you may burn the nipple skin). Put the neck of the bottle over the nipple, touching the skin all around to make an airtight seal (Fig. 4.4).

Hold the bottle steady. After a few minutes, the whole bottle cools and makes gentle suction, which pulls the nipple into the neck of the bottle. Sometimes when a woman first feels the suction, she is surprised and pulls away. You may have to start again. The warmth helps the oxytocin reflex, and milk starts to flow and collects in the bottle. Keep the bottle there as long as the milk flows. Pour out the breast milk, and repeat if necessary, or do the same for the other breast. After sometime,

(a) Put hot water into a bottle

(b) Pour out the water

(c) The mother holds the warm bottle over her nipple

Fig. 4.4. Warm bottle method to cure inverted nipple

the acute pain in the breasts becomes less, and hand expression or suckling may become possible.

How often a mother should express milk?: To establish lactation, to feed a low-birth-weight or sick newborn, mother should start to express milk on the first day within six hours of delivery, if possible. She may only express a few drops of colostrum at first, but it helps breast milk production to begin, in the same way that a baby suckling soon after delivery helps breast milk production to begin. She should express as much as she can, as often as her baby would breastfeed. This should be repeated at least every 3 hours, including during the night. If she expresses only a few times, or if there are long intervals between expressions, she may not be able to produce enough milk. Expression of breast milk is necessary for the following reasons:

1. To keep up her milk supply to feed a sick baby: She should express as much as she can, as often as her baby would feed.
2. To build up her milk supply, if it seems to be decreasing after a few weeks: Express very often for a few days (every ½-1 hour), and at least every 3 hours during the night.
3. To leave milk for baby while she is out at work: Express as much as possible before she goes to work to leave for the baby. It is also very important to express while at work to help keep up the supply.
4. To relieve symptoms such as engorgement or leaking at work: Express only as much as is necessary.
5. To keep nipple skin healthy: Express a small drop to rub on her nipple after a bath or shower.

How to Stimulate the Oxytocin Reflex

- Help the mother psychologically and build her confidence. Try to reduce any source of pain or anxiety. Help her to have good thoughts and feelings about the baby. Help the mother practically.
- Sit quietly and privately or with a supportive friend. Some mothers can express easily in a group of other mothers who are also expressing for their babies.
- Hold her baby with skin-to-skin contact (Fig. 4.5). She can hold her baby on her lap while she expresses. If this is not possible, sometimes even looking at her baby helps.
- Take a warm, soothing drink. The drink should not be coffee or tea.
- Warm her breasts. For example, she can apply a warm compress, or warm water, or have a warm shower.
- Stimulate nipples, gently pull or roll nipples with fingers.

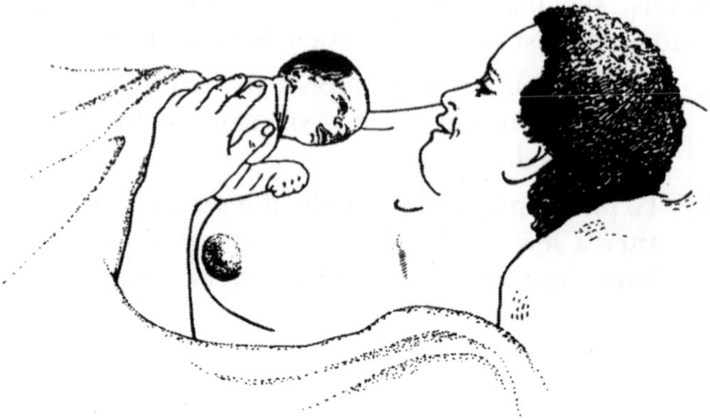

Fig. 4.5. Skin to skin contact helps in breastfeeding

- Massage or stroke the breasts lightly. Some women find that it helps if they stroke the nipple and areola gently with finger tip or with a comb. Some women find that it helps to gently roll their closed fist over the breast towards the nipple.
- Ask a helper to rub the back. The mother sits down, leans forward, folds her arms on a table in front of her, and rests her head on her arms. Her breasts hang loose, unclothed (Fig. 4.6). The helper rubs down both sides of the mother's spine. She uses her closed fist with her thumbs pointing forwards. She presses firmly making small circular movements with her thumbs. She works down both sides of the spine at the same time, from the neck to the shoulder blades for two or three minutes.

MANAGEMENT OF FLAT AND INVERTED NIPPLES

This problem is rare after the baby is born. This can however, make it difficult for the baby to feed. Flat inverted nipples occur, at the maximum, in only four to five per cent of all mothers. If this problem is noticed, hold the areola of the breast between the thumb and the first finger. If the nipple protrudes out, then baby will be able to feed without

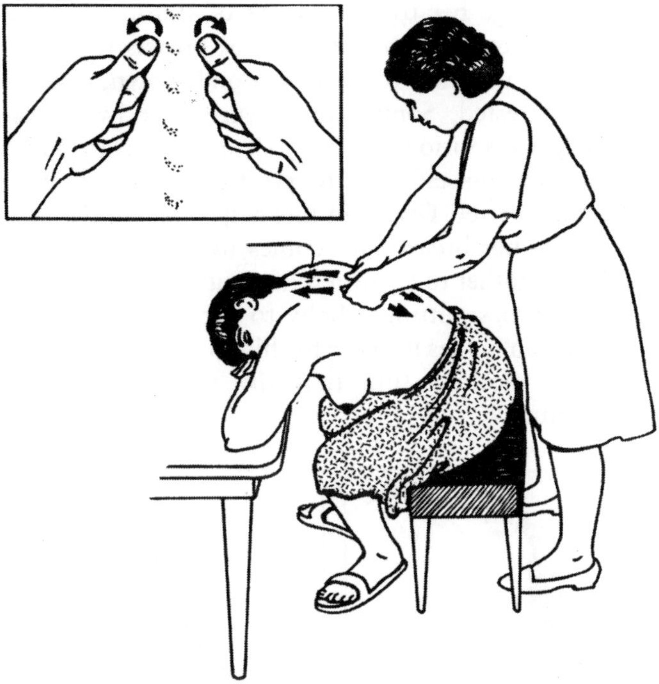

Fig. 4.6. Rubbing mother's back to stimulate oxytocin reflex

any assistance. If nipple does not protrude out, try wearing a shell.

- Antenatal treatment is sometimes not helpful. For example, stretching nipples, or wearing nipple shells does not help. Most nipples improve around the time of delivery without any treatment. Help is most important soon after delivery, when the baby starts breastfeeding. Build the mother's confidence. It may be difficult at the beginning, but with patience and persistence she can succeed. Her breasts will improve and become softer in a week or two after delivery. Her baby's suckling will help to pull her nipples out. Remember, a baby suckles from the breast—not from the nipple. Baby needs to take a large mouthful of breast.

- Encourage her to give plenty of skin-to-skin contact, and to let her baby explore her breasts (Fig. 4.7). Let him try to attach to the breast on his own, whenever he is interested. Some babies learn best by themselves. Help to position the baby. If a baby does not attach well by himself, help to position him so that he can attach better. Give him this help early, in the first day, before her breastmilk 'comes in' and breasts are full. Help mother to try different positions to hold her baby. Sometimes putting a baby to the breast in a different position makes it easier for him to attach. For example, some mothers find that the underarm position is helpful.

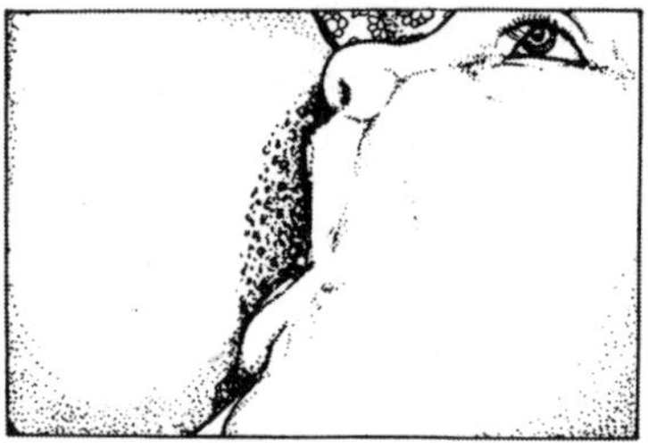

A baby well attached to mother

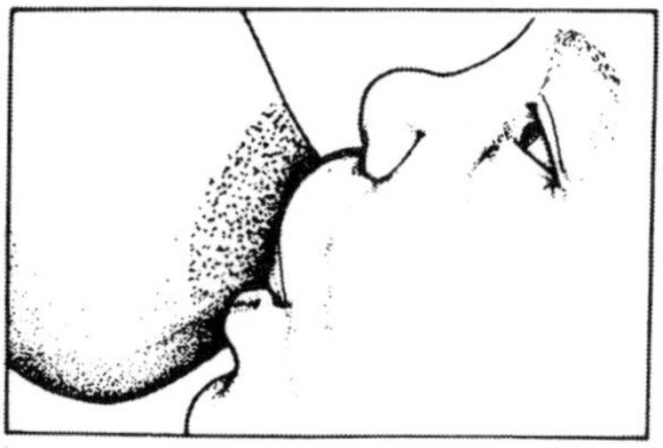

A baby poorly attached to mother

Fig. 4.7.

- Help mother to make her nipple stand out more before a feed. Sometimes making the nipple stand out before a feed helps a baby to attach. Stimulating nipple may be all that a mother needs to do. She can use either a hand-operated breast pump, or a syringe to pull her nipple out (Fig. 4.8). Sometimes, shaping the breast makes it easier for a baby to attach. To shape her breast, a mother supports if from underneath with her fingers, and presses the top of the breast gently with her thumb. She should be careful not to hold her breast too near the nipple. If it is acceptable to both partners, the woman's husband can suck on her breasts a few times to pull out the nipples.

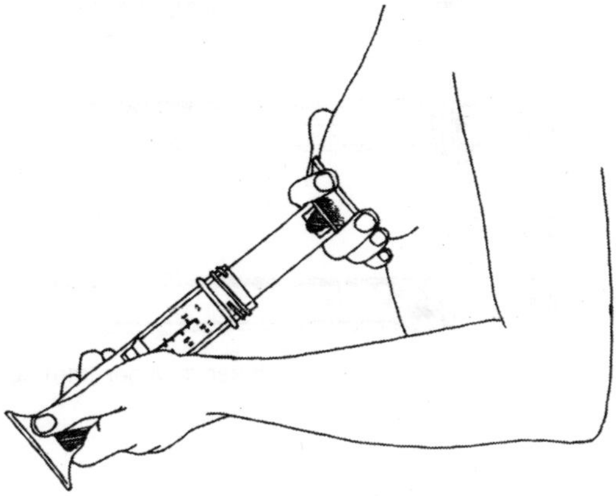

Fig. 4.8. Syringe breast pump

- If a baby cannot suckle effectively in the first week or two, help mother to express her milk and feed it to her baby in a cup. Expressing milk helps to keep breasts soft, so that it is easier for the baby to attach to the breast; and it helps to keep up the supply of breast milk. She should not use a bottle, because that makes it more difficult for her baby to take her breast. Express a little milk directly into her baby's mouth. Some women find this helpful. The baby gets some milk straight away, so he is less frustrated. He may be more willing to try to suckle. She should continue to give him skin-to-skin contact, and let him try to attach to her breast. Preparing and using a syringe for treatment of inverted nipples include three steps (Fig. 4.9):
  - (i) Cut syringe with blade.
  - (ii) Insert plunger from cut end.
  - (iii) Gently pull the plunger.

ENGORGEMENT OF THE BREASTS

The engorgement of the breasts results because of accumulation of milk in the breasts which causes pain and tenderness. Refer Tables 1, 2 and 3.

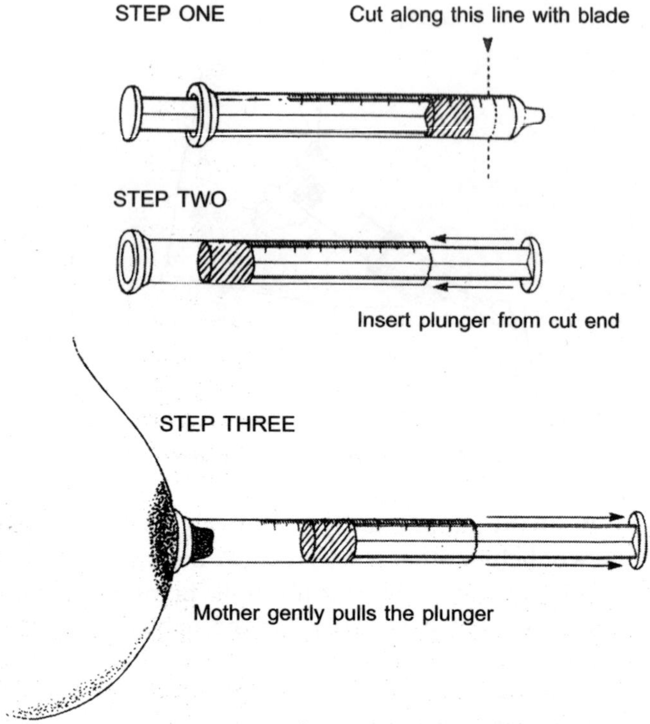

Fig. 4.9. Use a syringe for treatment of inverted nipples

Table 1: Summary of the difference between full and engorged breasts

Full Breasts	*Engorged Breasts*
Hot	Painful
Heavy	Oedematous
Hard	Tight, especially nipple, shiny and may look red.
Milk flowing	Milk not flowing
No fever	May be fever for 24 hours

Table 2: Causes and prevention of breast engorgement

Causes	*Prevention*
• Plenty of milk	
• Delay starting to breastfeed	• Start breastfeeding soon after delivery
• Poor attachment to breast	• Ensure good attachment
• Infrequent removal of milk	• Encourage unrestricted breastfeeding
• Restriction of length of feeds	

Table 3: Treatment of breast engorgement

Do not 'rest' the breast	
If baby able to suckle	Feed frequently, help with positioning
If baby not able to suckle	Express milk by hand or with pump
Before feed to stimulate oxytocin reflex	1. Warm compress or warm shower 2. Massage to neck and back 3. Light massage of breast 4. Stimulate nipple skin 5. Help mother to relax
After feed to reduce oedema	Cold compress on breasts

MASTITIS

If you have pain and swelling in one area of breast, you are perhaps suffering from mastitis. Refer Table 4 below to find out symptoms, causes and the treatment.

Table 4: Symptoms of blocked duct and mastitis

Blocked duct—Milk stasis	*——Non-infective mastitis——*	*Infective mastitis*
Lump	progress to	Hard swelling
Tender		Severe pain
Localized redness		Red Area
No fever		Fever
Feels well		Feels ill

Symptoms of Blocked Duct and Mastitis

Mastitis may develop in an engorged breast, or it may follow a condition called blocked duct. Blocked duct occurs when the milk is not removed from a part of the breast. The duct to that part of the breast is sometimes blocked thickened milk. The symptoms are a lump which is tender, and sometimes redness of the skin over the lump. The woman has no fever and feels well. When milk stays in a part of the breast, because of a blocked duct, or because of engorgement, it is called milk stasis. If the milk is not removed, it can cause inflammation of the breast tissue, which is called non-infective mastitis. Sometimes a breast becomes infected with bacteria, and this is called infective mastitis. It is not possible to tell from the symptoms alone if mastitis is non-infective or infective. If the symptoms are all severe, however, the woman is more likely to need treatment with antibiotics in consultation with a doctor.

Causes of Blocked Duct and Mastitis

The main cause of blocked duct and mastitis is poor drainage of all or part of a breast. Poor drainage of the breast may be due to infrequent breastfeed. As a result when the mother is very busy, baby starts feeding less often or feeds irregularly, and changed feeding pattern. The other causes include ineffective suckling if the baby is poorly attached to the breast, pressure from the tight clothes (usually bra which should be avoided during night) and pressure from the mother's fingers which block milk-flow during breastfeeding. The lower part of large breast drains poorly because of hanging.

Treatment of Blocked Duct and Mastitis

The most important part of treatment is to improve the drainage of milk from the affected part of the breast. Look for the cause of poor drainage and correct it in the following ways:

- Look for poor attachment.
- Look for pressure from clothes, usually tight ones if worn at night or pressure from lying on the breast.
- Stress and overwork of the mother which causes her to breastfeed the baby less often or for short duration.
- Trauma to the breast which damages breast tissue and causes mastitis.
- If there is a nipple fissure, it provides a way for bacteria to enter the breast tissue which can lead to mastitis.

Remedies for Blocked Duct and Mastitis

The main causes of blocked duct and mastitis is poor drainage of all or part of a breast. The following remedies are suggested:

- Frequent breastfeeding.
- Gently massage the breast while the baby is suckling.
- Apply warm compresses to the breast between feeds.

- Start feed on the unaffected breast.
- Breastfeed the baby in different positions at different feeds.

IF BABY CRYING TOO MUCH

Many mothers start unnecessary complements because they think that their baby 'cries too much'. They think that their babies are hungry, and that they do not have enough milk. However, complements often do not make a baby cry less. Sometimes a baby cries more. A baby who cries a lot can upset the relationship between him and his mother, and can cause tensions among other members of the family. An important way to help a breastfeeding mother is to counsel her about her baby's crying.

Reasons Why Babies Cry

Discomfort	:	dirty, hot, cold
Tiredness	:	too many visitors
Illness or pain	:	changed pattern of crying
Hunger	:	not getting enough milk, growth spurt
Mother's food	:	any food, sometimes cow's milk
Drugs mother takes	:	caffeine, cigarettes, other drugs
Oversupply of breast milk	:	causes colic – a gripping pain in a part of the intestinal tract which increases in intensity to a climax. It differs from continuous pain.

When a baby cries, the mother may feel guilty. She may feel angry with her baby. In such a situation, look for a cause. Learn about baby's feeding and behaviour. Following steps are advised:

1. *Hunger due to growth spurt*: A baby seems very hungry, possibly because he is growing faster than before. He demands to be fed very often. This is commonest at the ages of about 2 weeks, 6 weeks and 3 months, but can occur at other times.

2. *Mother's food*: Sometimes a mother notices that her baby is upset when she eats a particular food. This is because substances from the food pass into her milk. There are no special foods to advise mothers to avoid, unless she notices a problem. Babies can become allergic to the protein in some foods in their mother's diet. Soya, egg, and peanuts can all cause this problem.

3. *Drugs mother takes*: Caffeine in coffee, tea and colas can pass into breast milk and upset a baby. If a mother smokes cigarettes or takes other drugs, her baby is more likely to cry than other babies. If someone else in family smokes, that also can affect the baby.

4. *Oversupply*: This can occur when a baby is poorly attached. He may suckle too frequently or for too long and stimulate the breast too much, so that the milk supply increases. Oversupply can occur if a mother takes her baby off the first breast before he has finished, and makes him take the second breast. The baby may get too much foremilk, and not enough hindmilk. He may have loose green stools and a poor weight gain.

5. *Colic*: Some cry a lot without one of the above causes. The baby cries continuously at certain times of day, often in the evening. He may pull up his legs as if he has abdominal pain. He may appear to want to suckle, but it is very difficult to comfort him. Babies who cry in this way may have a very active gut or wind. This is called 'colic.' Colicky babies usually grow well and the crying usually becomes less after the baby is 3 months old. To bring up baby's milk, hold him upright, for example, in a sitting position, or upright against shoulder.

6. *High needs babies*: Some babies cry more than others, and they need to be held and carried more. In communities where mothers carry their babies with them, crying is less common than in communities where mothers like to put their babies down to leave them, or where they put them to sleep in separate cots.

MANAGEMENT OF SORE NIPPLES

Look for a cause:

- Check attachment.

- Examine breasts, e.g. engorgement, fissures, candida infection.
- Check baby's mouth for signs of candida and for tongue tie; and baby's bottom for candida rash.

Give appropriate treatment:

- Build mother's confidence.
- Improve attachment with the baby and continue breastfeeding.
- Reduce engorgement. Breastfeed frequently or express breast milk.
- Treat for candida if skin of the nipple and areola is red, shiny, or flaky. Check if there is itchiness, or deep pain, or if soreness persists.

Advise the mother to:

- Wash breasts only once a day, and avoid using soap or rubbing hard with a toe which can irritate the skin of breasts.
- Avoid medicated lotions and ointments without consulting a doctor.
- Rub expressed breast milk on areola and nipples.

WHY BABY REFUSES TO BE BREASTFED

Important Tips to Find out if a Baby is getting Enough Breast Milk or Not

1. *Check the baby's weight gain*: This is the most reliable sign. For the first six months, a baby should gain at least 500 gm in weight each month or 125 gm each week. If a baby gains less than 500 gm in a month, he is not gaining enough weight and consult a child specialist. If the baby is gaining enough weight, he is getting enough milk.

2. *Check the baby's urine output*: This is a useful quick check. An exclusively breastfed baby who is getting enough milk usually passes dilute urine at least 6-8 times in 24 hours. A baby who is not getting enough breast milk passes urine less than 6 times a day. If the baby passes less than 4 times a day, his urine is also concentrated, and may be strong smelling and dark yellow to orange, especially in a baby more than 4 weeks old. If a baby is passing plenty of dilute urine, he is getting enough breast milk.

Remember, these do not affect the breast milk supply:

- Age of mother
- Sexual intercourse
- Menstruation
- Age of baby
- Caesarean Section
- Many children

Important Reasons Why a Baby may not get Enough Breast Milk

1. ***Breastfeeding factors*:**
    - Delayed start
    - Infrequent short feeds
    - No night feeds
    - Poor attachment
    - Bottles, pacifiers
    - Complementary feeds
2. ***Mother's psychological factors*:**
    - Lack of confidence
    - Worry and stress
    - Dislike of breastfeeding
    - Tiredness
3. ***Mother's physical condition*:**
    - Contraceptive pill, diuretics
    - Pregnancy
    - Malnutrition
    - Alcohol, smoking
    - Retained piece placenta
    - Poor breast development

4. *Baby's condition*:

- Illness
- Abnormality

If Baby is Not getting Enough Milk

1. *Look for a cause*: Example history, breastfeeding factors, illness, abnormality, mother's nutrition, health or any breast problem.

2. *Build confidence and give support*: Help the mother to give her baby more breast milk and give her confidence that she can produce enough. Improve baby's attachment to breast. Breast will make more milk if baby takes more. Stop using bottles or pacifiers, reduce stress and anxiety.

3. *Help with less common causes*: If baby is ill or abnormal, consult a doctor. If mother is taking oestrogen pills or diuretic drugs, change.

4. *Proper follow-up*: Check daily, then weekly until baby is gaining weight. It may take 3-7 days for the baby to gain weight.

Helping a sick mother to breastfeed:

Sick woman	:	Encourage her to continue
If admitted to hospital	:	Admit baby with her
If she has fever	:	Give her plenty to drink
If she is unwilling to breastfeed	:	Help her to express her breast milk 4-hourly and feed the baby by cup
If extremely ill	:	Consider expressing her breast milk and feed the baby by cup
If mentally ill	:	Find a helper to care for mother and the baby together.

Mother's medications: Most drugs pass into breast milk in only small amounts. Few of them affect the baby. In most cases, to stop breastfeeding is more likely to be dangerous than the medicine. There are a few drugs which may cause side-effects. Problems are more likely in babies less than 1 month old, and less likely in older babies. However, it is usually possible to give the mother an alternative which is less likely to cause a problem, it is rarely necessary to stop breastfeeding because of a mother's medication. If a mother is taking anticancer drugs, it may be necessary to stop breastfeeding. If she is treated with radioactive substances, she should stop breastfeeding temporarily. A few drugs can cause side-effects which sometimes make it necessary to stop breastfeeding. If a mother is taking psychiatric drugs or anticonvulsants, these sometimes make breastfed baby drowsy or weak.

Some antibiotics should be avoided, if possible: Most antibiotics given to a breastfeeding mother are safe for her baby (preferably consult a doctor before treatment). It is better to avoid chloramphenicol, tetracycline, and metronidazole. Avoid giving a mother sulphonamide, especially if her baby is jaundiced. If treatment with cotrimoxazole, fansidar, or dapsone is necessary, give the drug and continue breastfeeding. Consider an alternative method of feeding if the baby is jaundiced, must consult a doctor in these cases. Drugs which decrease breast milk should be avoided, if possible. Avoid using contraceptives which contain oestrogens. Watch the baby for side-effects such as abnormal sleepiness, unwillingness to feed, and jaundice, especially if the mother needs to take the drug for a long time. If a baby has side effects and you cannot change his mother's medication, consider an alternative feeding method temporarily, if possible.

WHEN BABY REFUSES TO BREASTFEEDING

If the baby refuses to breastfeeding, treat or remove causes if possible. Help the baby to enjoy breastfeeding as explained in Table 5 below:

Table 5: Baby's refusal to breastfeeding

	Causes of refusal	*Remedies*
(i)	Illness, pain (due to bruise by wrong handling, sedation of drugs, blocked nose and sore mouth (due to thrush or teething)	Infections should be treated by antimicrobials and other therapy. Find a way to hold baby without pressing on a painful place. For thrush, treat with gentian violet or nystatin. For teething, be patient and keep offering the child the breast. Clear blocked nose. Offer short feeds more often for few days.

	Causes of refusal	Remedies
(ii)	Difficulty with breast-feeding technique	Adopt technique to breast feed. Reduce oversupply of milk as a result of poor attachment. Stimulate the breast so that it produces more milk than the need. This will help the baby to feed from both breasts at each feed. At the next feed, give the child the other breast. Do not shake breast. Do not apply pressure on the back of head which child is suckling.
(iii)	Changes which upset baby (especially aged 3-12 months)	Separation from mother, new carer or too many carers, mother ill or mastitis or menstruating and change in the smell of mother. Continue to sleep with child because night feeds may continue upto the age of 2 years.

Help the mother and baby to enjoy breastfeeding again: This is difficult and requires hard work. You cannot force a baby to breastfeeding. The mother needs help to feel happy with her baby and to enjoy breastfeeding. They have to learn to enjoy close contact again. Sometimes baby behaves in a way which makes his mother think that he is refusing to breastfeeding. However, he is not really refusing. When a newborn baby 'roots' for the breast, he moves his head from side to side as if he is saying 'no'. This is normal behaviour. Between 4 and 8 months of age, babies are easily distracted, for example, when they hear a noise, they may stop suckling. It is a sign that they are alert. After the age of one year, a baby may wean himself. This is usually gradual.

Table 6: Helping a mother and baby to breastfeed again

1. Keep her baby close—no other carers. Give plenty of skin-to-skin contact at all times, not just at feeding times. Sleep with her baby.
2. Offer her breast whenever her baby is willing to suckle, she should not hurry to breastfeed and offer her breast in different positions. When she feels her ejection reflex working, she can offer her breast then.
3. Help her baby to take the breast. Express breast milk into his mouth. Position him so that he can attach easily to the breast. Avoid pressing the back of his head or shaking her breast.
4. Feed her baby by cup. Give her own expressed breast milk, if possible. If necessary, give artificial feeds. Avoid using bottles, teats, pacifiers.

HERBS FOR BREAST CARE

Most of the ancient physicians were men who regarded women purely in the role of child producers and wet nurses. Now times have changed. Lady doctors and trained midwives are far kinder to suffering women, prescribing soothing lotions and potions. There are now a number of herbal preparations available which play a magic role in healing a disorder. Painful conditions of the breasts are very common among women. Any lump or bump in the breast should always be a sign to take immediate professional advice. Sore, cracked nipples are usually a result of breastfeeding, either because of the baby dragging at the nipple or because correct care is not being taken in washing and drying the breasts before and after feeding. Mastitis or hard breasts is an excruciatingly painful condition which causes inflammation as well as hardening of the breasts.

- Mallows are believed to increase the supply and flow of milk as are borage (pattbarchuri, patta ajwain), watercress (jalkhumbi), parsley (ajmod, prajmoda), fennel (saunf), anise (saunf), cumin, carrots, lentils, and fenugreek—all these have the added benefit of giving breasts an alluring roundness. Many of these herbs have the added benefit of counteracting post-natal depression.
- To prevent sore and cracked nipples which can make feeding a baby an unhappy experience, rub the nipples with a mixture of pure lemon juice and olive oil throughout the pregnancy. Whilst nursing, add a few drops of essential oil of geranium to a pot of cold cream and soothe the nipples with this.
- *Calendula* flowers are useful for clearing the skin of eczema, spots and grease. It is claimed to be rejuvenating. Its ointment may also help in treating breast disorders.
- *Marshmallow* is a herbal remedy for a greater flow of milk.
- To make a massage oil for the breasts, shake together 4 tablespoons each of apricot and wheat-germ oil. Warm it and massage painful breasts.

- *Camphor:* A few drops of oil of camphor (kapoor) mixed in two tablespoons of olive oil (jaitun ka tel) may be used to massage hard breasts but not when nursing.
- *Honey:* Mix honey with olive or lanolin (thick tacky fat available with dispensing stores or druggists which has a softening and moisturising effect, and is a good skin food) and use to anoint cracked nipples. Lanolin rubbed into the nipples soothes and softens, but before using, make sure you are not allergic to it.
- *Warm Poultices:* Standard and comforting remedy for mastitis. Baked potatoes, turnips, freshly cooked (not baked) beans pounded with olive oil, hot plasters and warm fomentations help.
- Take one teaspoon each of dried aniseed, and marjoram, half teaspoon each dried fenugreek and honey. Infuse the herbs in 600 ml boiling water for ten minutes. This potion improves the flow of breast milk.

5

Breast Function and its Disorders

At birth, the breasts consist of a simple system of ducts without alveoli and their development is, to some extent, exaggerated under the influence of maternal oestrogen. Within one or two weeks of birth, there are involutional changes. By the age of nine to ten years, the female breasts begin to enlarge (Fig. 5.1). The ducts and acini develop within the next three or four years, and by the time of the menarche, fat is deposited to make the breasts more prominent and round. Proliferation of the gland and enlargement of the breast continue until the age of 16 or 18 years. Pre-pubertal development is mainly the result of the action of oestrogen secreted by the ovary. The minimum hormonal requirements necessary for a mature non-lactating breast to grow are oestrogen, progesterone, GH and insulin. Prolactin is particularly important for mammary tissue to respond to oestrogen. The other important event needed for normal mammary development and function of puberty is deposition of adequate fatty tissue. The ducts and glands can expand in the tissue under hormonal stimulation.

The mature breast undergoes a cycle which corresponds to the ovarian cycle. Oestrogen stimulates the ductal elements, whereas oestrogen and progesterone stimulate glandular development and an increase in the water content of the breast. The breast as a whole increases in size during the week before menstruation mainly due to the congestion and oedema of the connective tissues between the lobules. The oedema is the part of the general tendency to water retention pre-menstrually, which probably explains the slight pre-menstrual pain and

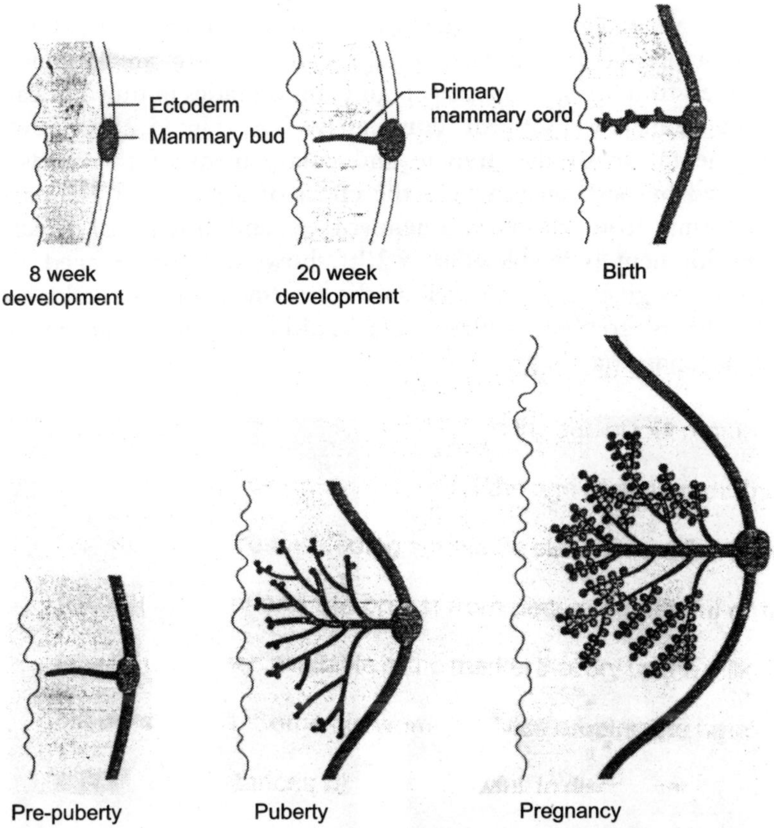

Fig. 5.1. Enlargement of breasts

tenderness in the breasts which many women experience. During pregnancy, there is an active development of both ducts and acini. The breasts enlarge and their vascularity is enormously increased. The acini secrete a small amount of glairy fluid—colostrum. The development of the breasts during pregnancy is caused by oestrogen which affects mainly the ducts, and by progesterone which affects mainly the alveoli. However, the lactation is dependant on an adequate diet.

The breasts respond by enlargement, and may become painful and tender. This may be undesirable in children, as well as old women. The areas of chronic mastitis react by forming cysts, an oedema may increase in size. Pigmentation of the breast areola, and production of a linea nigra are common sequels to oestrogen therapy. Pigmentation fades in time but can take years to disappear completely. The Fig. 5.2(a) shows pigmentation of the areolae and enlargement of the breasts caused by oestrogens where the effect of a girl aged 20 years suffering from primary amenorrhoea and absent of breast development is visible. Fig. 5.2(b) shows a teenager aged 18 who was given an oestrogen as the treatment of acne vulgaris. The breast areolae are almost black, although there is not much gynaecomastia.

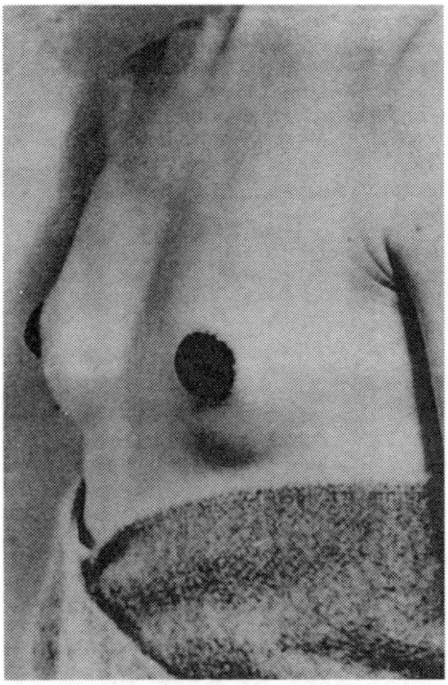

Fig. 5.2(a). Pigmentation of the areolae caused by oestrogen. The 20 year old had flat breasts and was suffering from primary amenorrhoea. Breast developed after 3 months treatment

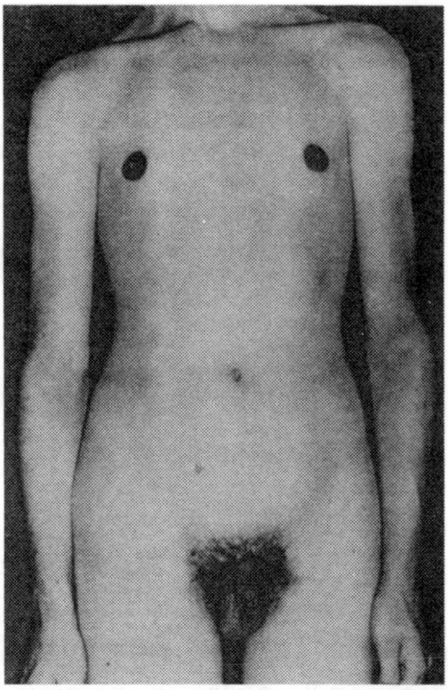

Fig. 5.2(b). A teenage boy of 18 was given an oestrogen treatment for acne vulgaris. The black breast areole were soon visible on his chest

LACTATION

No matter how far breast development proceeds during pregnancy, milk is never produced until the placenta is delivered or ceases to function. Lactation is inhibited during pregnancy by

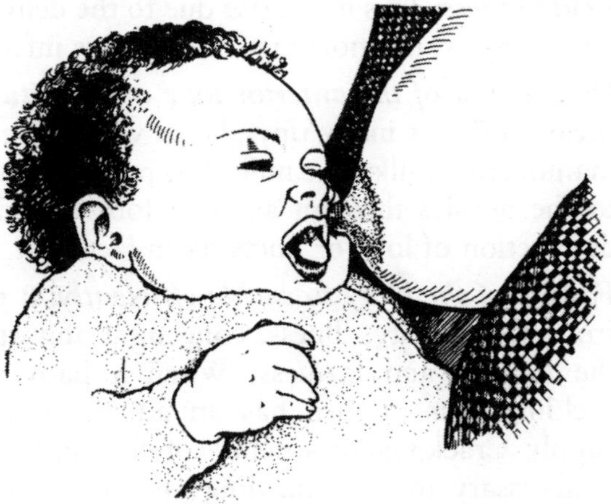

Fig. 5.3. Lactating mother

the action of placental oestrogen on the hypothalamus and anterior pituitary. Immediately after delivery, the inhibition is over and an outflow of prolactin initiates lactation. Once lactation starts, it is maintained by suckling or stimulation of the nipple (Fig. 5.3). Suckling stimulates the secretion of prolactin. Lactation continues almost indefinitely after pregnancy. The delivery of the milk from the nipple is brought about by contraction of myoepithelial cells around acini and ducts. These are stimulated by oxytocin in response to stimulation of the nipple—the let down reflex. This reflex also explains why suckling or handling of the breasts causes a strong contraction of the puerperal uterus.

ABNORMAL LACTATION (DEFICIENT LACTATION)

Abnormal lactation is caused due to the following reasons:

1. *Poor development of breast tissue*: The large breast is often the one with the most fat and the least glandular elements and does not always function well. The nipple may be small, flat or inverted and thus impede suckling.
2. *General ill-health and poor nutrition during pregnancy*: These may act over a long period and during pregnancy.

3. ***Acute illness***: This may arise due to the delivery shock, labour pains, haemorrhage and serious infections.
4. ***Destruction of the anterior lobe of the pituitary***: The breast contains many tiny glands whose function is to manufacture milk. The milk thus produced is conveyed to the nipples through anterior lobe and ducts. Any destruction of lobe or ducts harm lactation.
5. ***Failure of the baby to suckle efficiently***: It may result from prematurity, illness, congenital abnormalities of the mouth, and laziness. When a baby is lazy at suckling, this in turn has an adverse effect on the supply. Cracking and soreness of the nipples may make it necessary to stop suckling and this nearly always interferes with the supply of milk.
6. ***Failure of the baby to empty the breast***: A good supply of milk depends on emptying the breast fairly completely at each feed.
7. ***Psychological considerations***: Successful lactation depends on the mother's willingness to breastfeed and her determination to make it successful.

Treatment: The treatment of inadequate lactation depends mainly on ensuring that the mother is healthy in mind and body. Give attention to take care of the nipples and breasts. Maintain suckling reflex and undertake regular expression of colostrum from the breasts during the last few weeks of pregnancy. After delivery, at least 3 litres of fluid should be taken each 24 hours and if the baby fails to empty the breast at a feed, any remaining milk should be removed by pump or expression.

Bloodstained Milk

Bleeding from a cracked nipple is common due to contamination of the milk with blood from within the breast tissue. It may come from only one lobe or from the whole breast. A local lesion such as a duct papilloma results in bright red blood easily distinguished from the milk. A diffuse condition can result in the homogeneous mixture of the two fluids to produce 'brown milk'. It usually clears in a few days but if it persists, lactation has to be discontinued. A similar phenomenon, resulting in bloodstained colostrum, is sometimes seen during pregnancy.

Galactorrhoea

Galactorrhoea, or inappropriate lactation, is a continuous secretion of milk in the absence of pregnancy (Fig. 5.4). Although much commoner in women, it can occur in men. In women galactorrhoea may or may not be associated with amenorrhoea. It usually is when its cause is a significant disease or disturbance of the hypothalamic-pituitary system. The main causes of galactorrhoea are:

1. ***Physiological factors***: In nearly all women who have lactated, it is possible to express a little milk or allied secretion from the breasts for years afterwards, and especially premenstrually. This usually passes unnoticed until pain or other fleeting symptoms are noticed. Lactation is known to have occurred in virgins even the very young and the very old have repeatedly put a baby to the breast and have had an overpowering desire to feed it. Rare cases of this kind are reported mostly among primitive tribes.

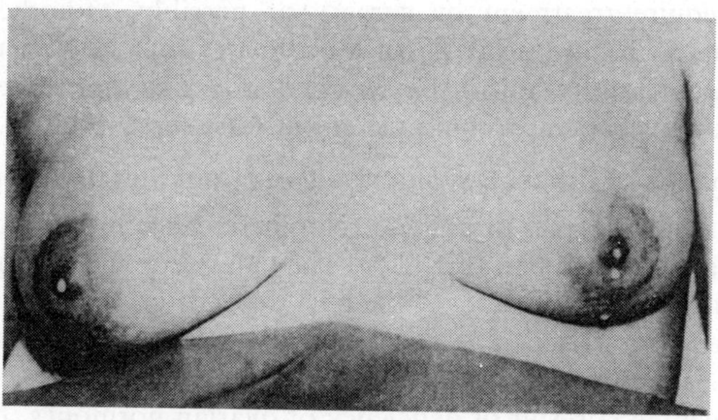

Fig. 5.4. 25 years old patient of galactorrhoea syndrome who became mother at the age of 22 and continued feeding her baby for 4 months. Her breasts are still active and secreting milk so far as shown in photograph above

2. ***Psychological factors***: Chronic emotional stress and psychiatric disorders.

3. *Hypothalamic and pituitary conditions*: It includes tumors of or in the region of the pituitary gland and midbrain basal meningitis, encephalitis, and functional disturbances.

4. *The chiari-frommel syndrome (galactorrhoea)*: It is characterized by lactation, amenorrhoea and superinvolution of the uterus dating from pregnancy. A 25-year-old patient who became mother at the age of 22 continued breastfeeding for four months and her breasts are still active secreting milk as shown in illustration.

5. *Drugs*: Such as reserpine, phenothiazine derivatives, including chlorpromazine, and other ganglion—blocking agents, can cause galactorrhoea, with or without amenorrhoea.

Diagnosis: The handling of the breast will reveal the cause in many cases. If galactorrhoea has been present for over six months and there is no obvious cause apart from hyperprolactinemia, then the possibility of a pituitary tumor must be considered.

Treatment: The treatment may be done according to the patient's age and desire for a pregnancy. Pituitary tumor produces neurological symptoms or other endocrine disorders and require treatment by surgery or possibly, radiotherapy. Patients who have no wish for a pregnancy may be kept under treatment and should be warned to take contraceptive precautions. Therapy continues for at least three months.

Anomalies of Breast Development and Function (Hypoplasia)

Varying degrees of underdevelopment of the breast are seen among young women (Fig. 5.5). They may seek medical advice on this account. The size of the bust depends on fat as much as on glandular tissue. The development of the nipple is the best guide. Hypoplasia of the nipples has the same causes and treatment as a result of deficiency of ovarian hormones. In this case, there is always other evidence of the deficiency such as amenorrhoea (Fig. 5.6) and genital underdevelopment. The defects in the gland are also responsible for this. The gland may be absent, rudimentary or insensitive to hormone stimuli.

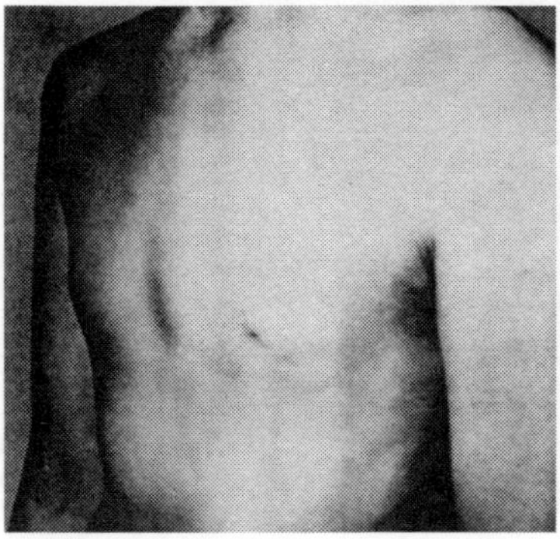

Fig. 5.5. Hypoplasia of the breast of a teenage girl whose both ovaries were removed at the age of 12. She had no breasts

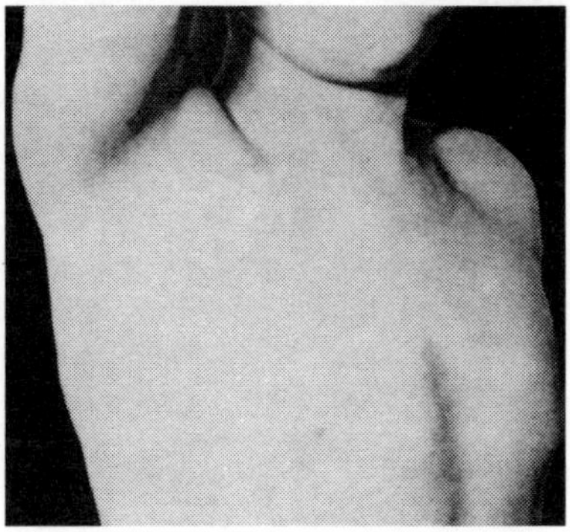

Fig. 5.6. Teenage girl suffering from amenorrhoea

Treatment: It is done by administering oestrogen and progestogen for several months (Figs. 5.7, 5.8 and 5.9). Although the hormone effect is temporary, the bust measurement does not usually deteriorate materially when treatment is suspended. If the menstrual and ovarian functions are normal, there is no point in administering oestrogen because the supply is already adequate and it is the breasts which are at fault.

Refer Fig. 5.5, a patient of Hypoplasia of the breasts, of a girl aged 19 years, who had both ovaries removed at the age of 12 years. The breasts had developed as a result of oestrogen therapy. In another case a patient, an apparent girl aged 16 years, complaining of primary amenorrhoea had underdeveloped breasts (Fig. 5.6). After the treatment, breasts started developing as a result of oestrogen therapy.

Thin patient should increase their weight. Physiotherapy, that is, local massage, exercise for the pectoral muscles and measures designed to improve the blood supply may prove valuable. Suction bust developers in the market are useless. Plastic surgery, i.e. the placing of non-irritant prostheses deep to the breasts can give satisfactory results. Surgeons prefer to graft fat, with its overlying skin, from another site (such as the buttocks).

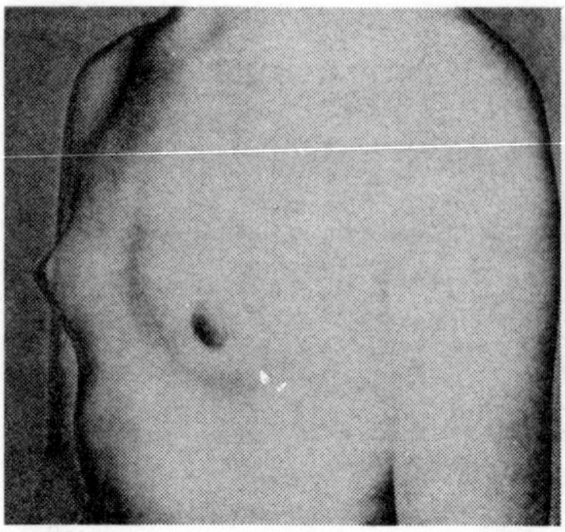

Fig. 5.7. The breasts started developing as a result of oestrogen hormone therapy

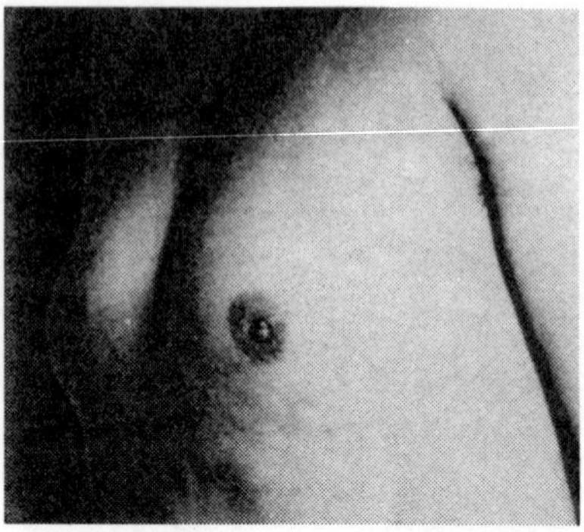

Fig. 5.8. Enlargement of breasts in a male due to oestrogen

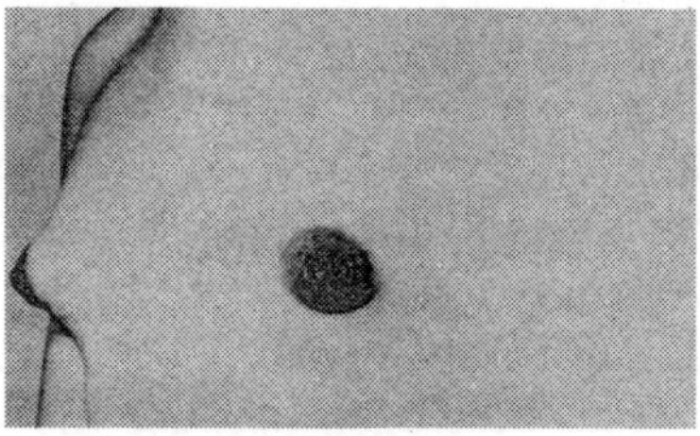

Fig. 5.9. The undeveloped breasts developed with oestrogen treatment in 4 months

Breast Asymmetry

The breasts are similar to most paired organs in the sense that they are rarely equally developed. Even if they look the same, their function is unequal when they lactate. The baby prefers one to the other because he obtains more milk more easily. Often the breasts are obviously different in size and, since both are subject to the same hormone stimulus, the fault is always inherent in the target tissues. Endocrine treatment is valueless but plastic surgery can offer reduction in size of the larger organ and sometimes enlargement of the smaller.

Retracted (Inverted) Nipples

Acquired retraction of the nipple developing in later life is a sign of cancer. Here retraction is being considered only as a developmental anomaly caused by fibrous bands fixing the base of the nipple to the underlying fascia. Plastic surgery treatment for this condition is unsatisfactory. Generally, there is no justification for treating retraction of the nipple unless the woman is pregnant. Pregnancy itself often brings about considerable improvement in the anatomy and, at that time, physiotherapy and the wearing of special shields are more likely to be effective.

Accessory Breasts and Nipples

The axillary tail of spence is well-developed in some women and may result in axillary pain and swelling premenstrually or during lactation. Sometimes there are accessory breasts, but more commonly there are accessory nipples only. These are usually found on the nipple line which extends from the anterior fold of the axilla to the pubic spine. Small pigmented moles on this line are nearly always accessory nipples and are extremely common. No treatment is necessary.

Hypertrophy of the Breasts

Hypertrophy of the breasts is not common. It affects the glandular tissue and not the nipples. Its cause is unknown. It is nearly always bilateral and often first appears at puberty. The breasts enlarge progressively and can weigh as much as 6-13 kg each. They undergo further hypertrophy in pregnancy but they do not lactate. In extreme cases, they interfere with walking. Treatment consists either of supporting the breasts with a special brassiere or of performing a plastic surgery. Such operations are best deferred until the woman is more than 20 years of age. Fig. 5.10 shows an adolescent hypertrophy of breast of a 13-year-old girl who

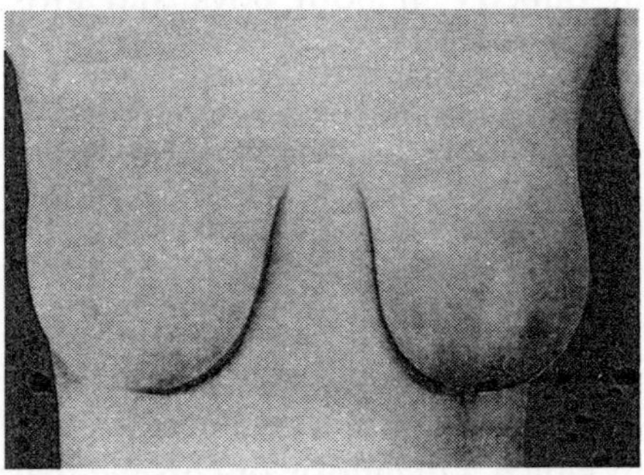

Fig. 5.10. Adolescent hypertrophy of breast. Breasts of a girl aged 13 who had started menstruation when she was 10.

had been menstruating from the age of 10. Another Fig. 5.11 exhibits breasts of a 28-year-old woman—a case of bilateral hypertrophy of breasts.

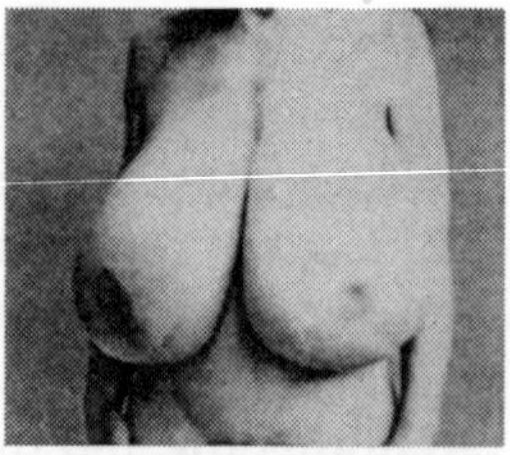

Fig. 5.11. A case of 28 years old woman – Bilateral hypertrophy. The marks on the breasts were caused due to pressure of brassiere on oedematous

Pendulous Breasts

After child-bearing and lactation, and with advancing age and obesity, the breast loses its firmness and shape. Sometimes, it becomes so pendulous as to be an embarrassment. The treatment immediately after lactation is to support the breast and to encourage pectoral exercise. A plastic surgery gives good results.

Neonatal and Adolescent Mastitis

The breasts of male or female babies sometimes become enlarged and hard within 3 or 4 days after birth. The condition is associated with congestion and activity of the primitive ducts and is related to the withdrawal of the influence of maternal oestrogen. The baby attempts to lactate at the same time as its mother lactating. Indeed, a discharge may occur from the nipple, the so-called 'witch's milk'. No treatment is required; the condition gradually resolves of its own. Adolescent mastitis is a nodular painful enlargement of the breast that sometimes occurs at puberty in both boys and girls. It reflects the upsurge in pituitary activity.

Fibroadenosis (chronic mastitis)

This condition is also known as chronic cystic hyperplastic mastopathy or fibroadenosis. The breast is tender on examination and has an ill-defined nodularity. Histologically, there is overgrown fibrous tissue with distortion and cystic dilatation of ductules. Duct and gland tissues are increased in amount. In the majority of cases in which the complaint is painful breasts, and in which a diagnosis of chronic mastitis is made, the lesion is in the psyche rather than in the breast. Patients are frequently unmarried and approaching menopause; they tend to be over-anxious and to have a fear of cancer.

Diagnosis and Treatment

It is essential not to overlook an early cancer and if there is doubt, the opinion of an expert and possibly biopsy are necessary. Every tumor, no matter how benign it may appear, requires removal treatment, should be by reassurance, by brassiere and by leaving the breasts alone, not by mastectomy. When it affects younger women, pregnancy can be curative. If hormone therapy is given for fibroadenosis of the breast, then a combined oestrogen progestogen pills are given cyclically to suppress disease.

6

Breast Cancer in Women

Cancer of the breast is one of the leading causes of cancer mortality in Indian women. Data emerging from the six population-based cancer registries of the National Cancer Registry Programme of Indian Council of Medical Research (ICMR) highlights the high incidence of breast cancer. Breast cancer ranks first in Delhi and Mumbai and second in Chennai, Bangalore, Bhopal and Barshi. The relative frequency of breast cancer appears to be on the rise in this data.

TECHNIQUE OF SELF-EXAMINATION

This is a three-step method:

1. Inspection in front of mirror with the arms by the sides, straight up in the air, overhead and on the hips, looking for changes in contour, skin colour or texture and nipple changes.
2. Palpation in the shower.
3. Palpation in the supine position on a couch or a bed. Palpation can be performed in several directions; horizontal or vertical, radial or circular. A study of effectiveness of these three patterns determines that vertical pattern is the most thorough in examining breast tissue. Diagnostic tests are of two types: Non-invasive tests are conducted by mammography and ultrasound whereas invasive tests include aspiration cytology, core needle biopsy and open biopsy. There are indications for mammography in both screening and diagnostic setting. Patients with tumors or areas of

asymmetry, nipple discharge, skin retraction or axillary lymphadenopathy should be evaluated by mammography. Ultrasound is most helpful in differentiating cystic and solid areas. Masses less than 5 to 10 mm may not be visualized. Masses in fatty breasts are also difficult to visualize. Its advantages are that there is no radiation and it is entirely painless.

Among invasive tests include the following:

1. ***Aspiration cytology*** involves use of five needles with syringe to aspirate cells from suspicious area and fix them immediately for cytological evaluation. However, specific histological diagnosis may be impossible to maintain architectural patterns with aspiration. A limitation of this technique is to accurately determine oestrogen and progesterone receptors on a specimen of such small size. Core needle biopsy uses large bore needles. Aspiration is performed with better accuracy and ability to perform receptor determinations. These biopsies can be done stereotactically or with ultrasound guidance.
2. ***Open biopsy*** (Excisional biopsy) requires a curvilinear incision along langer's lines using local anesthesia on an out-patient basis and frozen section may be performed and a portion of specimen can be preserved for oestrogen and progesterone assay. The treatment of breast cancer by early detection through screening mammography has undoubtedly played a role in mortality reduction, chances for better life have been observed by early detection of breast cancer. It is concluded that avoiding post-menopausal obesity and regular physical activity are simple measures that seem to reduce breast cancer risk.

CANCER IN WOMEN

In women, the two most likely places where cancer may develop are the breasts and the uterus. Both areas are easily examined and every woman owes it to herself to have this done periodically. Far too many women die from cancer for no other reason than being careless, too modest or too sensitive.

SELF-EXAMINATION

Every young woman should be taught to examine her own breasts after each menstrual period. Before dressing, she should lie on her back with a small pillow under the shoulder on the side she is examining. This tends to flatten out the breast and makes the detection of any tumors. Then using the soft, flat part of her fingers on the opposite hand, she should gently palpate or feel the breast tissues, outlining the normal curves of the breast and notice whether any small masses are developing either within the breast tissue itself or up in the armpit. She should then place the pillow under the other shoulder and carry out the same procedure, using the other hand. Next she should stand or sit before a mirror and carefully note the size and shape of the breasts, preferably with her arms above the head, at the same time leaning slightly forward. By this means, she will soon become very familiar with the normal shape and can readily point out to the doctor any change that may have occurred. If she finds anything unusual, report it to doctor at once, for the earlier such abnormalities are discovered, the better the chances for her complete cure. Most tumors of the breasts are not due to cancer, but no one can tell what is going on without examining these tissues.

NINE STEPS TO BREAST SELF-EXAMINATION DETECTING CANCER OR TUMORS

1. Carefully examine the breast before a mirror for symmetry in size and shape. Note any puckering or dimpling of the skin or retraction of the nipples (Fig. 6.1(a)).
2. Now raise arms overhead and again study breasts in mirror for the same signs (Fig. 6.1(b)).
3. Recline on a bed with a flat pillow or folded bath-towel under the shoulder on the same side as the breast to be examined (Fig. 6.1(c)).
4. To examine inner half of the breast, the arm is raised over the head. Begin at the breastbone and in a series of steps, palpate the inner-half of the breast (Fig. 6.1(d)).

5. Carefully palpate the area over the nipple with flats of fingers (Fig. 6.1(e)).
6. Completion of examination of lower half of breast (Fig. 6.1(f)).

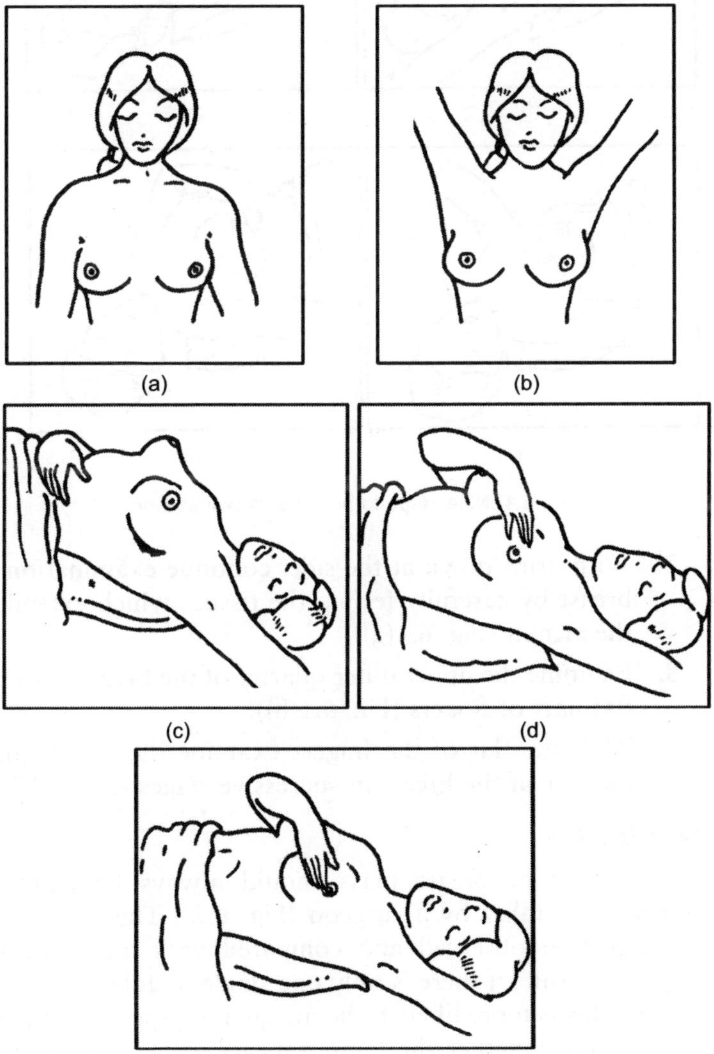

(e)

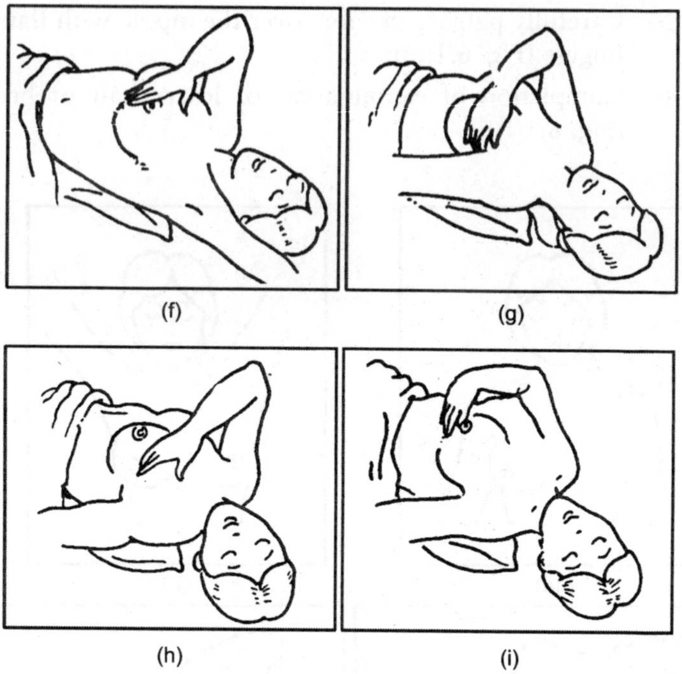

Fig. 6.1. Nine steps to breast self-examination

7. With arms down at the side, continue examination of breast by carefully feeling the tissues which extend to the armpit (Fig. 6.1(g)).
8. Examine the upper outer quarter of the breast with the flat part of fingers (Fig. 6.1(h)).
9. With the flat of the fingers examine the lower outer quarter of the breast in successive stages (Fig. 6.1(i)).

BREAST TUMOR

Any tumor or breast mass should always be carefully examined, preferably by a surgeon (Fig. 6.2). The size of the mass should be observed and compared with any previous findings. As a rule, if there is only one single nodule or lump in the breast, this is more likely to be malignant, especially if there is no pain. But whether the lump appears to be malignant or benign, it should always be removed and examined by a

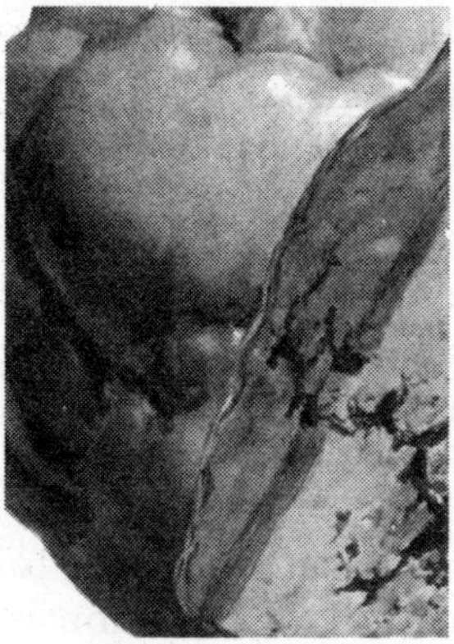

Fig. 6.2. Cell tumor

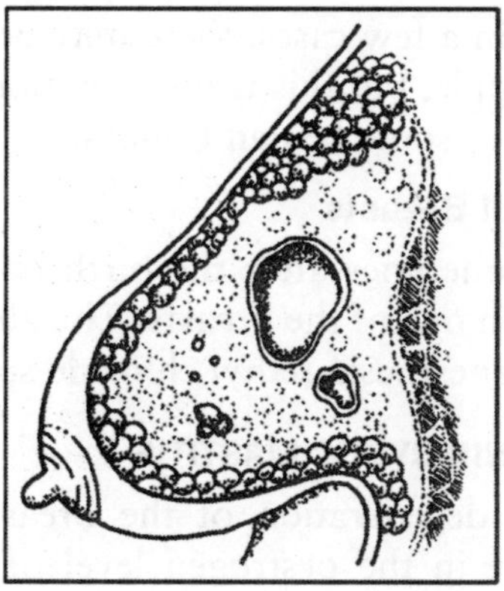

Fig. 6.3. Breast tumors are removed by surgery

pathologist (Fig. 6.3). This is a minor surgical procedure. The tissue so removed is usually examined by frozen section. If any malignancy is found, the whole breast and all the lymph nodes in the armpit are then removed. If the cancer appears to have extended into the neighboring lymph nodes, the patient should be given extensive radiation therapy to the whole area. However, this can usually be prevented by early diagnosis.

IT IS BREAST CANCER

Although a malignancy may develop in any part of the breast, the majority of cancers occur in either the upper portion of the breast, toward the shoulder, or else close to the nipple. Breast cancer may occur at any time of life. But it is more common between thirty-five and sixty-five years of age. After the age of sixty-five breast cancer is rare. When cancer is present in the breast, there is usually one hard single lump which may be fixed to the surrounding tissues (Fig. 6.4). Usually there is no

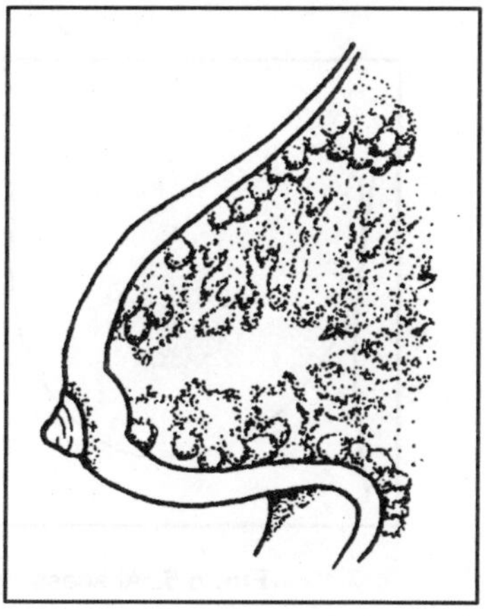

Fig. 6.4. Rapidly growing cancer

pain. In a few cases, there may be slight bloody discharge from the nipple, but this is not common. A slight discharge may also occur in some benign tumors.

Painful Breasts

Sometimes after the birth of baby, a painful abscess may form in one of the breasts. The abscess should be opened under local anesthesia (ethyl chloride spray) and the pus drained out.

CHRONIC CYSTIC MASTITIS

A degeneration of the breast ducts or tubules is due to change in the oestrogen level of the blood. This condition is often seen in women over thirty-five. They usually complain of mild tenderness in the breasts just before the menstrual period. The patient has an aching and heavy feeling in the breasts with perhaps an occasional stinging pain. These benign cysts usually feel spongy or rubbery, which is quite different from the hard toughness of most cancers of the breast (Fig. 6.5). These lesions tend to fade away at the menopause and usually cause no more trouble. In younger woman, it is most important to do a breast biopsy operation, although it is always wise to observe the condition for a few weeks to detect any changes that may be taking place.

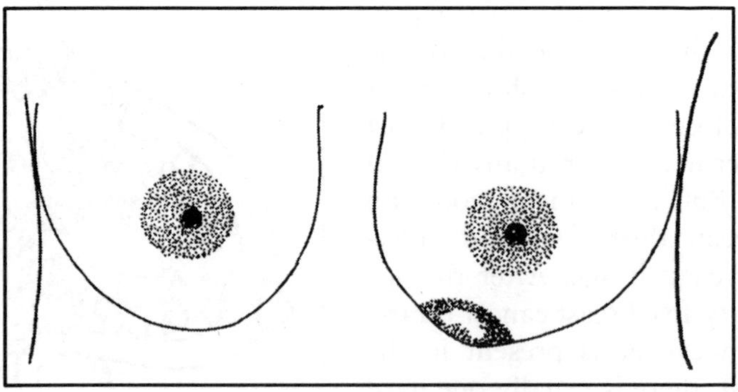

Fig. 6.5. Abscess due to chronic cystic mastitis

Causes of Nipple Discharge

Galactorrhoea	*Other Types*
Pregnancy and childbirth	Cancer
Neonatal	Intraductal papilloma
Breast manipulation	Ductal ectasis
Surgery	Gross cystic change
Stress	Infection
Drugs*	
Sellar tumors	
Hypothyroidism	
Chronic renal disease	

* Phenothiazines, rauwolfia alkaloids, tricyclic antidepressants methyldopaoral contraceptives.

HOW TO HELP YOUR FRIEND OR SISTER TO EXAMINE HER BREAST

Not necessary as a routine, only if the woman is concerned for postnatal, examine before breastfeeding. Do the examination gently and modestly:

1. Inspect your breast without touching. Look for size and shape of breast, size and shape of nipple, dripping milk and see if breasts are full, soft, engorged. Inspect fissures, white spots, redness due to inflammation or infection and scars (breast surgery, previous abscess, etc).
2. Ensure if you have noticed anything wrong; if "Yes" point the place, if it is necessary to palpate.
3. Palpate gently all parts of both breasts. Use the flat of your hand (fingers together and straight). Do not pinch or poke. Watch for signs of pain or tenderness. Feel for generalized fullness, hardness, engorgement, localized hardness, hot areas, lumps, etc.
4. Watch how easily your nipples stretch out (protract). Place finger and thumb on the areola either side of nipple and try to stretch the nipple out.
5. Talk to the mother about what you have found abnormal. Use confidence and support skills. Do not say anything critical, and do not tell things that will worry her when you are examining a patient.

HOW TO EXAMINE PALPATES OF BREAST

With the patient seated, the examiner palpates the supra- and infraclavicular area and the anterior cervical chain for enlarged node (Fig. 6.6(a)). With the patient seated, the examiner squeezes the breast between the fingers of both hands while pulling it outward in order to palpate lesions close to the chest wall (Fig. 6.6(b)). With the patient seated, the examiner palpates the breast tissue with the flats of the fingers of both hands in clockwise direction, leaving no area untouched (Fig. 6.6(c)). With the patient supine and the arm extended in order to flatten the breast, the tissue is palpated with the fingers by pressing it gently against the chest wall, again using a palm that will cover the entire breast, including the axillary tail (Fig. 6.6(d)). The procedure is repeated with the patient's arm at her side to relax the pectoral muscles (Fig. 6.6(e)).

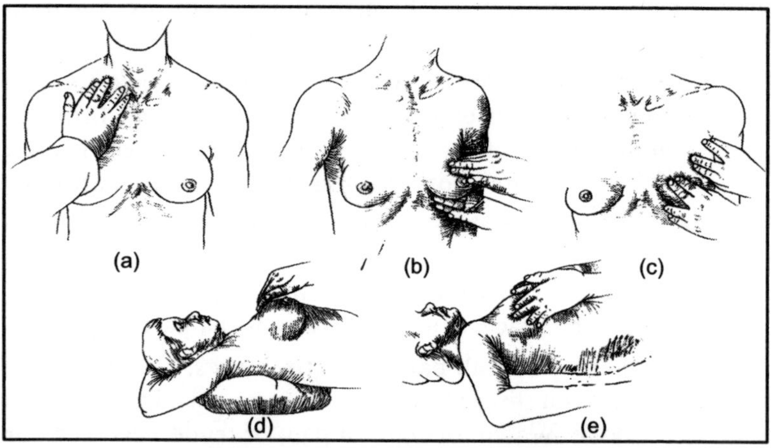

Fig. 6.6. To examine palpates of the breast

CANCER OF THE CERVIX

Pelvic cancer is a vicious killer of women today. Cervix is easily treated, provided the diagnosis is made early. Every woman aged twenty years and older should have a pelvic examination and a pap smear at least once each year or every six months if there is any suspicion of cancer or a history of malignancy among the other members of the family. Any watery discharge which continues more than a day or two should be investigated. In some cases, it could mean cancer (Fig. 6.7). The same is true of unexpected bleeding, particularly if the bleeding or spotting follows intercourse or douching. Most of these cases

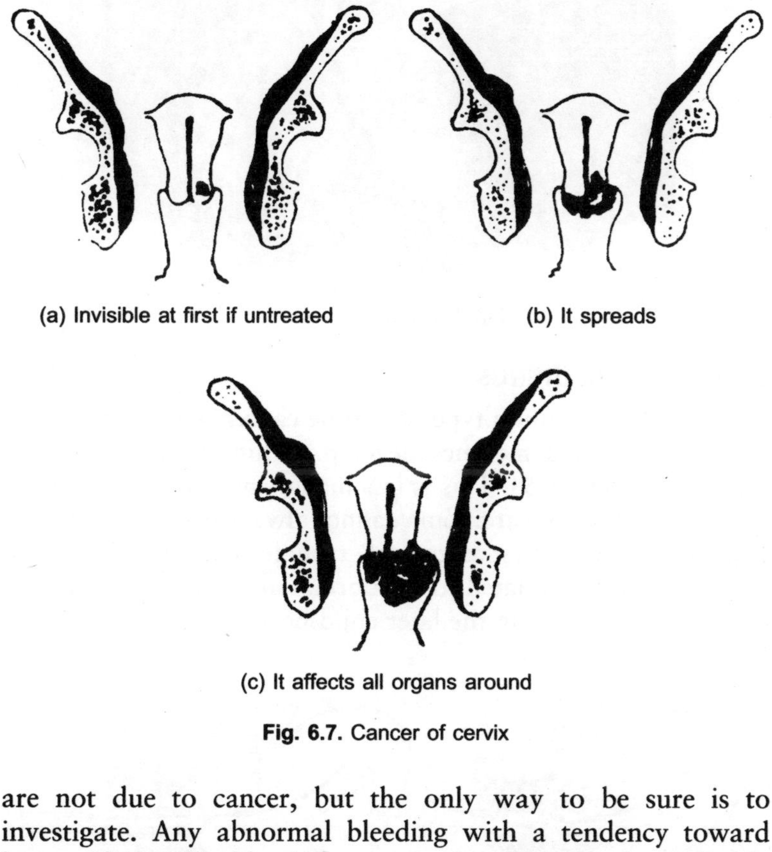

(a) Invisible at first if untreated

(b) It spreads

(c) It affects all organs around

Fig. 6.7. Cancer of cervix

are not due to cancer, but the only way to be sure is to investigate. Any abnormal bleeding with a tendency toward haemorrhage should raise a woman's suspicions immediately (Fig. 6.8). Modern treatment for uterine cancer consists of implanting a small amount of radium within the cervical canal followed later by heavy doses of radiation therapy to the whole pelvic area. Performing a hysterectomy, removing the uterus, cervix, ovaries, and tubes are the treatments in case of confirmed disease.

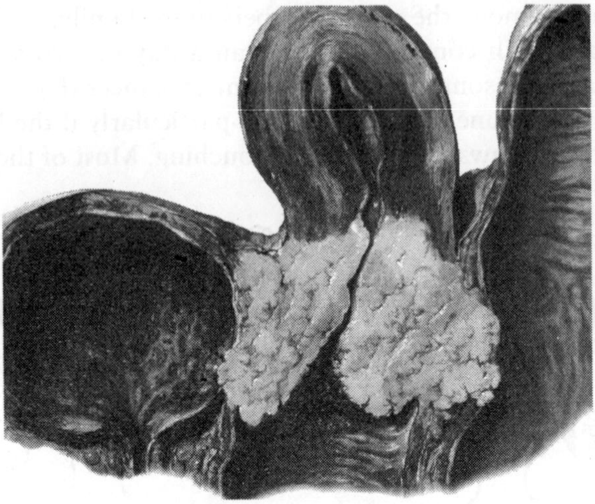

Fig. 6.8. Cervical cancer

CANCER OF THE UTERUS

It is a less common type of uterine cancer, known as fundal carcinoma, may sometimes develop within the cavity of the uterus itself (Fig. 6.9). This is less malignant than cancer of the cervix. This type of carcinoma cannot always be detected by the pap smear. The first signs of trouble may be a sudden haemorrhage, not related to the normal menstrual cycle. This is more likely to occur in the later child-bearing years. If cancer is

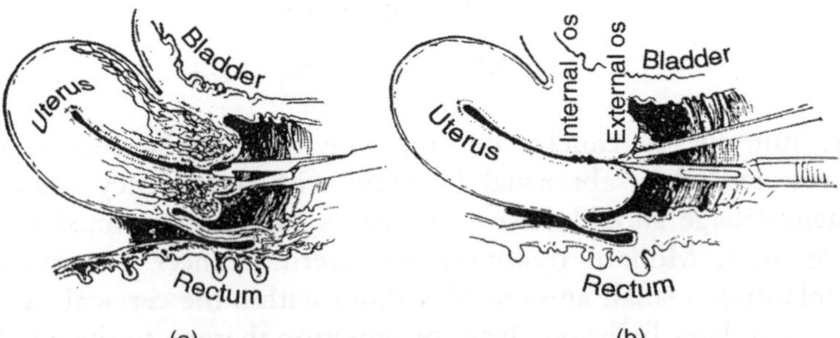

Fig. 6.9. Uterus cancer
When cancer is suspected, determine it by simple biopsy and treat immediately: Two steps (a and b)

found, a hysterectomy should be done without delay. The cancer cells may find their way into the abdominal cavity and may spread first to the local tissues of the pelvis by invasion, and then eventually throughout the whole body by the process known as metastasis (Fig. 6.10(a) to (e)). Widespread radiation therapy is recommended for treatment (Fig. 6.11).

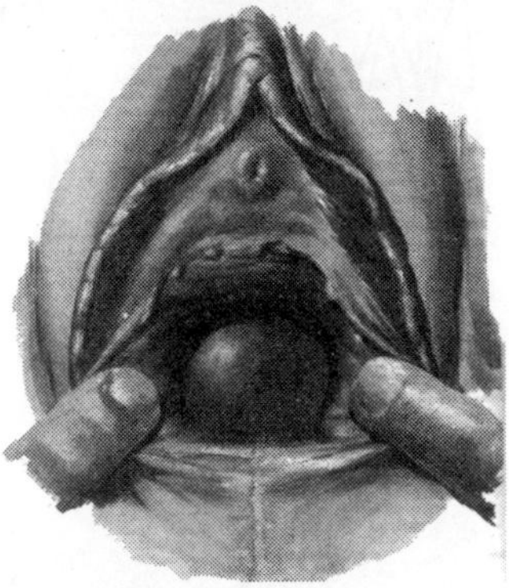

(a)

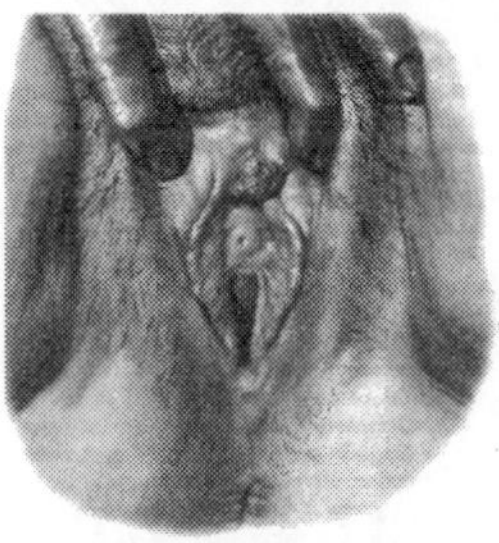

(b)

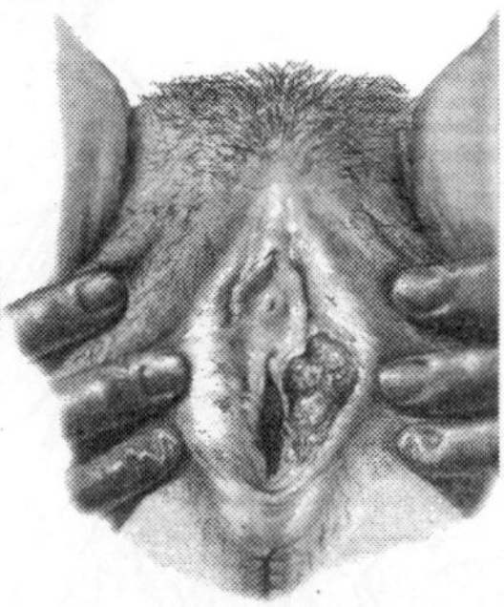

(c)

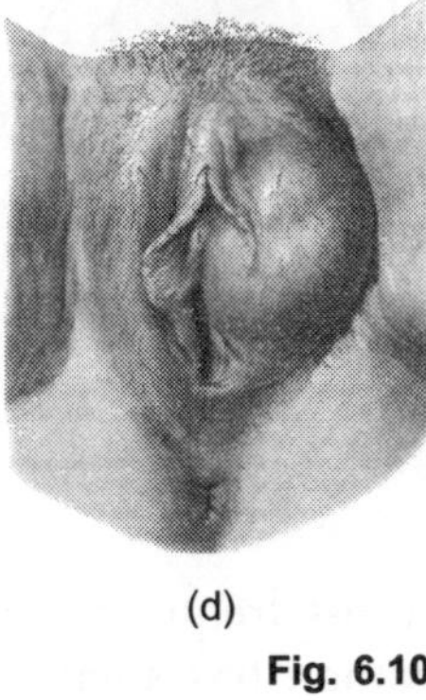

(d)

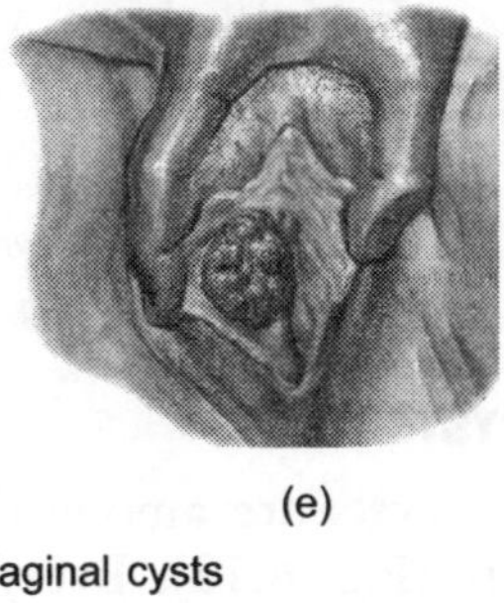

(e)

Fig. 6.10. Vaginal cysts

(a) Examining uterus cancer

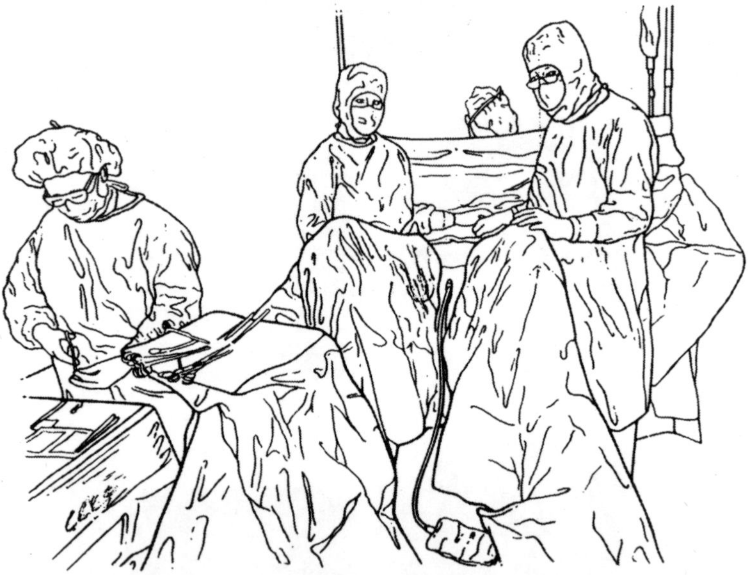

(b) Pelvic surgery

Fig. 6.11

OVARIAN CYSTS

Ovarian cysts are among the most frequent tumors in the female body (Fig. 6.12). Every woman has small cyst on the

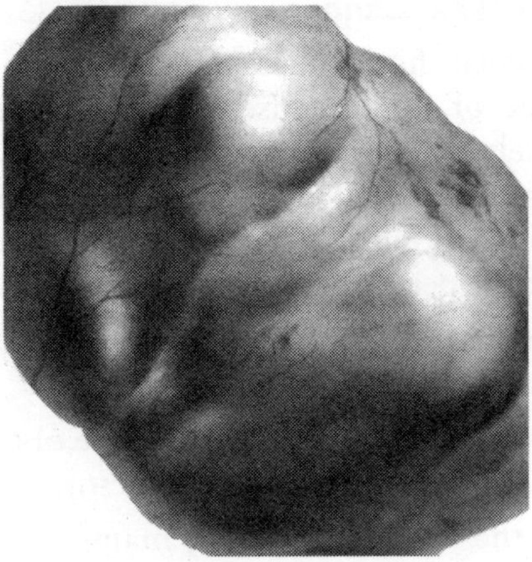

Fig. 6.12. Ovarian cyst

ovary which may disappear spontaneously. But when an ovarian cyst becomes large and causes distension of the abdomen and pressure on organs, e.g. the bladder or rectum, it should certainly be removed. Cancer may sometimes develop in the wall of an ovarian cyst, as a result cyst may then spread to other nearby organs (Fig. 6.13). Ovarian cysts should be removed by surgery without delay.

Fig. 6.13. Ovarian cancer

Screening for Breast Cancer

- All women should be taught self-breast examination by the age of 20, because of the changes which occur routinely in reponse to the hormonal sequence of a normal menstrual cycle. Breast examination is most effective during the follicular phase of the cycle and should be performed monthly.
- All women over the age of 35 should have an annual breast examination.
- A baseline mammogram should be obtained by the age of 40, or earlier, if high risk factors are present.
- From the age of 40 to 50, mammography should be performed every two years in low risk women and every year in women with significant risk factor.
- Annual mammography should be performed in all women over the age of 50.

Endometriosis

It is a troublesome condition arising because small bits of endometrial tissues have found their way outside the uterus into the abdominal cavity, causing inflammation and painful adhesions. The patient may then complain of painful menstrual periods.

The endometrial implants may also form tiny cystic structures which begin to secrete and grow. The patient may complain of a mild aching in the lower part of the pelvis. These cysts continue to enlarge (Fig. 6.14). This pain is likely to be aggravated by sex contact. The situation becomes worse just before and during menstruation. This situation tends to get steadily worse until the menopause, after which it usually may disappear. However, the painful adhesions caused by endometriosis may be relieved only by surgery.

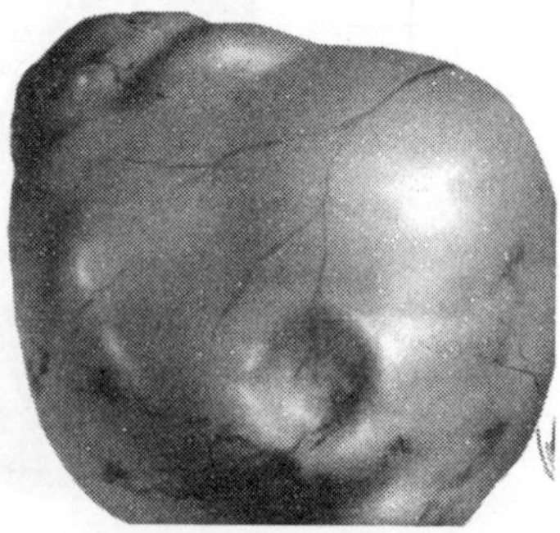

Fig. 6.14. Dermoid cyst

7

Mammography

The technique of breast radiography, discovered as long ago as 1953, has three radiographic methods—film mammography, film screen mammography and xeromammography.

FILM AND FILM-SCREEN MAMMOGRAPHY

This technique was based on the principles of soft-tissue radiography, which are:

- Low kV to produce soft radiation in order to differentiate between soft tissues with similar absorptive properties.
- High mA to give contrast and sufficient blackening of the film.
- Low filteration of the X-ray beam so that the soft radiation is not removed.
- Collimation of the beam to reduce scatter.
- Compression of tissue to reduce thickness and movement and consequently to reduce scatter and motion blurring.
- Small focal spot to reduce geometrical blurring.
- Short object-film distance to reduce geometrical blurring, the breast being in contact with the film.
- Long anode-film distance again to reduce geometrical blurring.
- The use of fine-grain (non-screen) film to give maximum detail.
- Hand processing to give optimum processing results.

Originally tungsten anodes were employed. These had the disadvantage of emitting X-radiation. In order to overcome this problem molybdenum targets were developed. Xeroradiography allows penetration of dense breasts also.

XEROMAMMOGRAPHY

Xeromammography is an electrostatic process rather than a chemical process. The principles of xerography and its applications in breast examination have been well-described, basically as a charged selenium plate is discharged by X-radiation in proportion to the amount of radiation reaching the plate. The xeroradiographic image has several characteristics, e.g. it has a wide recording latitude, enabling the skin, nipple, base of breast and even chest wall to be seen equally clearly on a single image. Other imaging modalities are:

Thermography

This modality is useful in the examination of the breast. The technique is non-specific. It may demonstrate thermal and vascular abnormalities which are not specific to any disease process but may be found in malignancy, in benign diseases and even in normal breasts.

Diaphanography

There is a resurgence of interest in transillumination of the breast as a diagnostic technique.

Ultrasound of the Breast

Realistic ultrasonic examination of the breast has become feasible since the development of grey-scale imaging. The breast may be examined using linear or compound scanning methods. The sonographic appearance of breast lesions are dependent on the density of the lesions in the breast.

1. *Cysts*: give rise to smooth, well-defined, anechoic, transonic lesions with distal enhancement and refractive edge shadowing (Fig. 7.1).

2. *Fibroadenoma*: presents a smooth, rounded or lobulated lesion with homogeneous or varying echo levels sometimes associated with posterior enhancement. There are varying degrees of attenuation if coarse calcifications are present (Fig. 7.2).

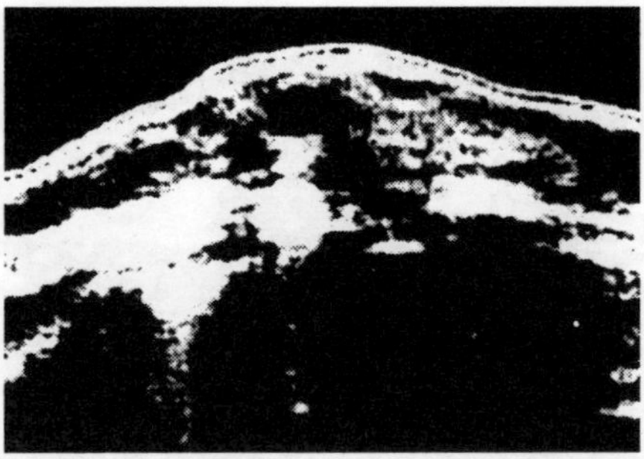

Fig. 7.1. Cysts

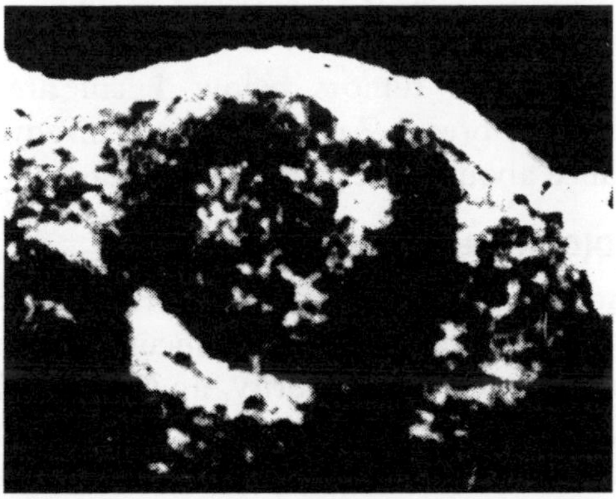

Fig. 7.2. Fibroadenoma

3. ***Carcinomas***: usually possess well-defined, irregular anterior and lateral margins but a poorly defined posterior margin which becomes more obvious with increasing intensity of the ultrasound. A distal shadow is seen as a result of attenuation of the beam (Fig. 7.3). The malignant mass shows low-level echoes as compared with normal breast tissues, circumscribed cancers (usually of the colloid or medullary variety), however, may display a homogeneous (echo) pattern and posterior enhancement, thus simulating benign lesions. There are several disadvantages of the modality. Not all cancers cause attenuation, especially colloid and medullary cancers, and as such the very lesions are difficult to diagnose radiographically. Fine micro calcification of the type seen in malignancy cannot

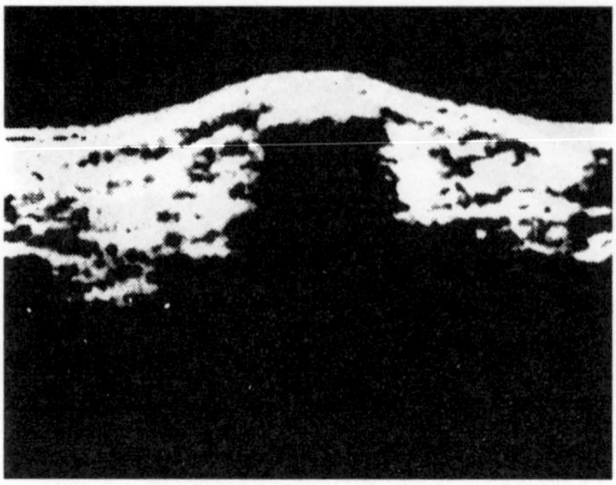

Fig. 7.3. Carcinomas

be demonstrated and tumors below 1 cm are difficult to demonstrate in the breast. Another serious disadvantage is the need to produce about 20 scans of each breast.

NORMAL RADIOGRAPHIC APPEARANCE

In the adolescent, the glandular portion of the breast is dense and clearly separated from the subcutaneous fat (Fig. 7.4). With increasing age and maturity and especially following pregnancies, an increasing amount of fat deposition occurs within the mature, glandular portion of the breast (Fig. 7.5). Blood vessels and trabeculae are more easily seen and the margins of the breast disc become less well-defined. In the menopausal and post-menopausal age groups, the glandular tissue is replaced by fat, eventually giving a fatty atrophic breast in which vessels and trabeculae are seen and lactiferous ducts

Fig. 7.4. Immature adolescent breast

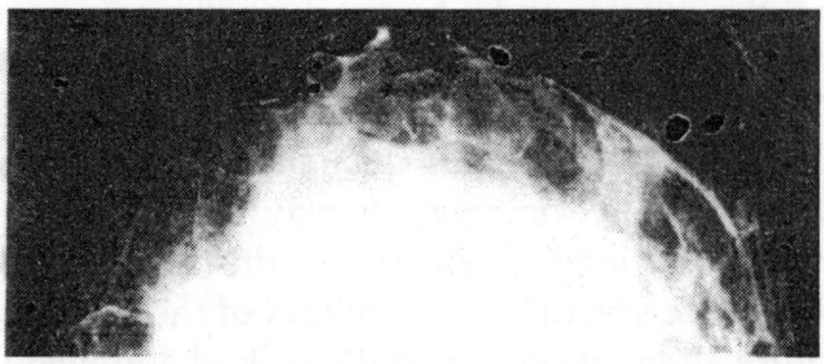

Fig. 7.5. Mature glandular breast

are also seen beneath the nipple. Cancer can be easily seen in such breasts as a result of the natural contrast provided by the fat.

ABNORMAL APPEARANCES OF LESIONS

The various abnormalities found on mammography are:

Malignant Lesion

The malignant lesion is usually of high density, the opacity nearly always showing a non-homogeneous texture as a result of asymmetric growth of the tumor which are usually irregular. These irregularities take the form of long thin spicules (Fig. 7.6). Rarely the tumor is well circumscribed and smooth in outline. This type of change is found in colloid or mucoid carcinoma and in intracystic carcinoma.

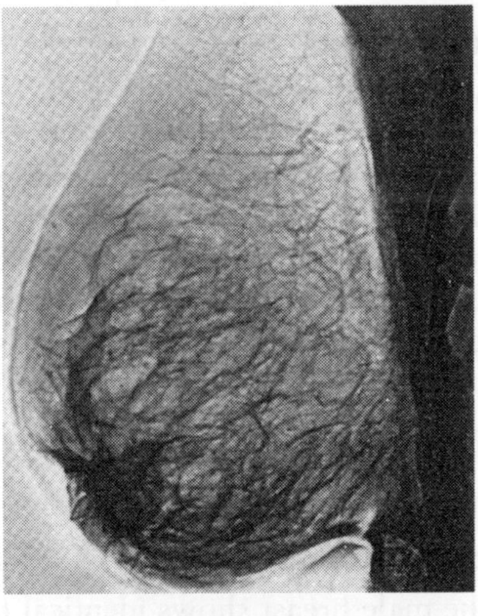

Fig. 7.6. Xerogram, subareolar abscess

Benign Lesion

Benign lesions are of variable but homogeneous density. They usually have low density as compared with malignant lesions. The cysts are often more dense than the glandular tissue. A fibroadenoma is usually of similar density to the surrounding glandular tissues, whereas cysts are often a little more dense than the glandular tissues. However, giant fibroadenomata can show great density, whereas small cysts may show low density. Lipomata are constantly transradiant. Acute inflammatory processes and acute abscesses are ill-defined but an abscess tends to become circumscribed with increasing chronicity (see positive xerogram in Fig. 7.6).

Changes in Breast Architecture (Thickening of the breast)

Lactriferous ducts may be straightened or enlargement of ducts may occur due to intraduct tumor or distal blockage by the cancer. Nipple retraction occurs. Skin dimpling over the tumor is a common occurrence. In benign disease, breast architecture is deformed rather than disrupted or destroyed. Ducts may also be displaced but the most common ducts abnormality is enlargement due to dilation of the duct or to thickening of the duct wall.

Vascularity of the Breasts

Among about 45% of normal women, the left breast is more vascular than the right breast and it is difficult to assess the hypervascularity of the left breast if only marginal changes are present. However, increased vascularity of right breast should always be regarded as significant as only in about 5% of normal women is the right breast more vascular than the left. Increased size and number of veins frequently occur in association with malignancy but the changes are not invariable.

BREAST LESIONS

Breast lesions are the following:

Carcinoma of the Male Breast

Cancer of the male breast shows identical features to those of the female breast. Microcalcification is not as common, however, smooth circumscribed carcinoma is relatively more common in the male.

Paget's Disease of the Nipple

This condition is usually associated with breast cancer. Radiologically, there may be an irregular mass with or without microcalcification or microcalcification may be the only sign of malignancy.

Cystosarcoma Phylloides

This is a cystic, fleshy tumor. It is usually a large, smooth, dense, lobulated lesion which may contain coarse irregular flake-like calcification.

Fibroadenosis (Fibrocystic disease; mammary dysplasia)

This benign condition is extremely common and is related to the menstrual cycle, usually combined with a palpable nodularity or thickening and tenderness of breast tissues. The syndrome may be associated with any radiological appearance of the breast, including completely fatty breasts, fatty glandular breasts with or without cysts or associated prominent ducts.

Sclerosing Adenosis (Lobular sclerosis, lobular fibrosis)

It may present as a hard mass with or without associated breast discomfort.

Duct Ectasia (secretory disease, periductal mastitis & plasma cell mastitis)

This is an idiopathic inflammatory condition of the breast ducts. The condition followed by inflammation may be present with nipple discharge at varying appearances, including serous, milky and bloodstained discharge. A painful limp is common. Radiologically, the ducts are enlarged and sometimes transradiant due to increased fat content. The condition may give rise to fat necrosis.

Gynaecomastia

In the normal male breast, the mammogram shows a small, faint, linear density beneath the nipple. A low density opacity of varying size is seen. In this condition its differentiation from cancer of the male breast and its associations with systemic disease is seen.

Galactography–Contrast Examination of the Breast

Contrast examination of the lactiferous ducts is a well-established supplementary method of investigation of breast disease. The commonest indication is a serious bloodstained nipple discharge. It also occurs frequently with duct ectasia and during later stages of pregnancy and lactation. Greenish and brownish nipple discharge are associated with duct ectasia and cystic disease. The condition should be thoroughly investigated even in the absence of palpable abnormality—this may lead to breast cancer.

Pneumocystography

A breast cyst with the main indication of bloodstained fluid on aspiration of a cyst. This indicates the presence of an intra-cystic papilloma or carcinoma. Pneumocystography demonstrates the presence, position and extent of an intracystic tumor preoperatively and usually a diagnosis of benign or malignant tumor can be made.

Indications for Mammography

The use for mammography is in the investigation of symptomatic patients as a complementary method to clinical examination. Its clinical diagnosis is to confirm patients with a palpable lesion either in the same breast or in the opposite breast. It is a useful complementary method of examination in patients with vague breast symptoms, eczema of the nipple or nodular breasts. Accuratic assessment of the response of the primary breast cancer is possible in cases treated with radiotherapy or chemotherapy. Finally, unsuspected cancers of the breast may be found on mammographic screening.

How to Conduct Mammography Test

Women feel hesitant about going for tests. Sometimes, a check-up is the only thing that stands between timely intervention and fatal disease and save your life.

Mammography is a technique of taking soft tissue X-rays. Two films of each breast are taken after adequate compression under an acrylic sheet by a radiologist.

1. *When should you get it done*?: If you have pain, discharge or a lump in the breast, if you would like a routine screening, if you have a family history of breast cancer, if you are undergoing hormone replacement therapy (HRT) which incidentally should always be in consultation with your doctor and if a lump is felt during self-examination or felt by the doctor during routine examination.

2. *What should you keep in mind*?: Mammography should preferably be done after the month's menstrual cycle.

3. *What part of the body will be checked*?: The breasts and the armpits.

4. *What will be your body position during the test*?: You will be standing with your breast resting on a flat platform before the equipment.

5. *What can you expect during the procedure*?: The breast is placed on the platform and flattened slightly for a very short period of time by an acrylic sheet. This may be slightly uncomfortable for some women, but is largely bearable.

6. *What will the results show*?: The presence of tumors (which can be investigated for benignity or malignancy). It will also indicate calcifications and cysts, as well as abnormal distortion of the internal structure, all of which need further investigation.

7. *Dimensional echocardiography*: is second test for women because many are increasingly prone to cardiac problems and valve lesions. It checks the structure of the heart—the walls, chambers, valves and the aorta and pulmonary artery. Also that the pericardium and the blood flow gradients. It should be done under advice from a doctor.

8. *The position during the test*: will be lying on back, then turned to left side. After the application of contact jelly to facilitate the procedure, probes will be applied to the chest. The results will show any abnormality in the structure of the heart and its parts. It will help in the diagnosis of congenital heart disease, abnormalities of the pumping action of the heart, movements of the heart muscles and defects of the heart valves and their movements.

9. *To prepare for your mammogram*: Schedule your appointment when your breasts are least tender to lessen the discomfort from the X-ray. By all means, avoid the week before your menstrual period. Go dressed for the examination. Wear a two-piece outfit—a skirt and blouse, a salwar-kameez or a two-piece suit so that you'll need to remove only your top.

Don't use deodorant, lotion or powder under your arms or near your breasts—this shows up in X-rays. When the doctor is reading the mammogram, make sure he or she has copies of your prior mammograms so that he or she can compare the pictures and look for changes.

10. *For a more comfortable mammogram*: Take a normal pain medication like an analgesic, beginning the day before your mammogram. Cut down on caffeine and salt one to two weeks before a mammogram. Practise deep breathing or meditation during the procedure. During the mammography, decrease your perception of pain by thinking about something else or focusing on a point in the room. Relax your muscles as the technician positions your arm and breast. It will get over quicker if you are less tense and don't try to position yourself. Speak up if you feel unbearable pain.

Mammography Limitations

Solid and cystic masses cannot be differentiated. Intracystic lesions cannot be diagnosed. Young breasts have dense fibroglandular parenchyma (loosely packed tissue filling) which obscures masses. Fibrocystic mastitis may mask the margins of a lump, and as a result, benign lumps may appear malignant. Overlapping structures may limit complete visualization of a mass. Evaluation of a tender breast is difficult and often inadequate.

Remedies: Ensure that the doctor follows the correct mammography technique with the right amount of compression. Sonography is a useful adjunct, especially to evaluate dense young breasts. Histopathological examination of the aspirate (fluid) drawn from the diseased part, using ultrasound or mammography control, would help in diagnosis of disease.

A Pap Test

Don't panic if your doctor asks you for a pap test, for timely diagnosis and to prevent cancer. The test will be carried out by a gynaecologist. As a part of a routine gynae checks up in the case of menstrual complaints, if there is a constant discharge from the vagina, if you bleed after intercourse, if your doctor thinks your cervix is unhealthy or that there are lesions or growths on it. All sexually active women must take an annual series of three tests. Remember to abstain from sexual intercourse for 24 hours prior to the smear. Do not douche or use a vaginal pessary for 48 hours prior to the procedure. The cervix, and sometimes the vagina or uterine cavity will be checked during the test.

Sonography of the Pelvis

Sonography relies on sound waves to draw a visual picture with the help of an in-built computer, unlike in X-rays. The procedure has no hazard of radiation and this makes it safe during pregnancy. It should be done in case of lower abdominal pain, menstrual disorders, infertility, vaginal discharge and for routine screening. During pregnancy, the procedure is used to confirm the pregnancy to diagnose multiple pregnancy, to observe the growth of the foetus, to ascertain the position of the placenta, to detect external abnormalities of the foetus and to estimate the weight of the foetus by sonography.

What should you keep in mind?: That your bladder is full which pushes the intestines up to facilitate viewing of the relevant parts. Do not pass urine for at least two hours before the test and drink as much water as you can. The uterus, the ovaries, cervix and bladder are usually checked by sonography. To conduct test, after the application of contact jelly, a sensor probe is moved over the lower abdomen. It is a painless procedure. Sonography of the upper abdomen is done using sound waves to form a visual picture of the organs of the upper abdomen. You should get it done when you suffer from abdominal pain, prolonged fever and inexplicable weight loss. There are many other conditions related to the liver, gall bladder, pancreas, spleen, kidneys and lymph glands in which sonography is useful as a diagnostic tool. Keep in mind that you need to fast for three hours prior to the procedure. The upper abdominal organs—liver, kidneys, spleen, pancreas, gall bladder and retroperitoneum are checked in this test. The sonography is a painless procedure. After application of contact jelly, a transducer is moved over the abdomen and the organs are viewed with the help of sound waves which observe structural abnormalities in the organs of the upper abdomen.

Endoscopy

Endoscopy is a procedure to visualise internal parts of the body through endoscopes. The term 'endoscopy' is used for a variety of such procedures as gastroscopy (for the stomach), duodonoscopy (for the duodenum), colposcopy (for the colon or large bowel), laparoscopy (for the abdomen, etc.). With the advent of miniaturization and fibre-optics, it is possible to have a look at almost every approachable organ of the body.

Laparoscopy

It is the introduction of a telescope into the abdomen to see the intra-abdomen and pelvic structures and organs, and also to carry out surgery in the abdomen and pelvis. The test is carried by a gynaecologist. A laparoscopy may be used to diagnose infertility, endometriosis, chronic pelvic pain, ectopic pregnancy, genital tuberculosis, pelvic inflammatory disease, the beginning of ovarian cancer and to evaluate the response to treatment of the same. Uterus, tubes, ovaries and surrounding pelvic peritoneum intestines are checked in this process by lying on your back with knees flexed and legs apart. During the procedure, under general anesthesia, a small one cm cut is made below the umbilicus, the abdominal cavity is filled with carbon dioxide gas and a telescope is introduced. Next, a light source is connected to the telescope in order to make it possible to see the intra-abdominal organs. In case of emergency, carry out surgery at the same time.

Hysteroscopy

Hysteroscopy means an introduction of a telescope into the uterine cavity after dilatation of the cervix to make room for this introduction. The test is carried by a gynaecologist. When the threads of the IUCD are not visible but are known to be within the uterine cavity, this test is done for removal of fibroids and for tubal ligation by blocking the tubal openings for family planning. The uterine cavity is checked by this test. Lying on your back with your knees flexed and legs apart under local or general anesthesia, a direct visualization of the uterine cavity lining and scraping is removed for biopsy.

Colposcopy

Colposcopy means direct visualization of the outside of the cervix (exocervix) under microscope. Get it done if your pap smear is abnormal or the cervix seems unhealthy or where lesions on the cervix cannot be pinpointed. The cervix of the body is checked during the test, lying on your back with knees flexed and legs apart. During the procedure, the colposcope is focused on the cervix to enable visualization, then the abnormal area is marked out. Next, acetic acid solution is (one per cent) put on the cervix and the junction of the aceto-white and non-white area is marked out. The treatment should be done by an experienced gynaecologist.

Mammography Attributes Early Diagnosis of Breast Cancer

Cancer site incidents in women: One out of every nine women who live to the age of 85 suffer from breast cancer. In view of the increasing incidents, the data indicate an improvement. The survival rate of localized breast cancer has risen from 78% to 93%, this is attributed to earlier diagnosis because of the greater utilization of screening mammography.

Out of nearly 70% cancer site incidence reported among women, the cases of breast cancer is the leading site of all cancers as detailed below:

	Cancers reported	*Deaths reported*
Breast cancer	33%	18.5%
Rectum and colon	13%	11.3%
Lung cancer	12%	22.5%
Uterus cancer	8%	4%
Ovary cancer	4%	5.3%

8

Yoga for Bust Development

Yogasanas exercise the body muscles and internal organs, increase body strength and provide relaxation. These stimulate the flow of blood to all parts of body. This also helps in the elimination of accumulated toxins and waste-products which clog the vital capillaries and the lymphatic and nervous channels. Some of the asanas are especially beneficial for strengthening the bust, help both underdeveloped and overdeveloped breasts.

YOGA FOR BOTH SEXES

Yoga is equally useful for men and women. It is more useful to women than men, but women lag behind in taking regular exercise. Exercise of the breast is important for women, helps to remove congestion of blood and tones up the muscles.

Selection of the Place

For practising yoga, one must have a peaceful, clean, airy place where there is enough privacy and the least of disturbance due to noise, visitors and other factors. The best place for women for practising yoga exercises would be the home. One may also enjoy yoga at a peaceful place on the bank of a river, or in a park or temple, big rooms or halls specially engaged for that purpose. But practising yoga individually at home is to be preferred wherever possible.

What to Wear while doing Yoga

This would depend on the climate, social norms, individual liking and preferences. While practising yoga in the open, the clothing should be sufficient to protect the body from cold. In pleasant weather especially while practising in a room just an underwear may suffice. In hot weather, a short or loin cloth may be all that is necessary. The clothes should cover the body neither too much nor too scantily. There should be no feeling of discomfort due to tight or too many clothes.

YOGA EXERCISES (POSTURES) FOR BREAST DEVELOPMENT

10-Minute Practice of Surya Namaskar

(Refer 10 positions of Fig. 8.1)

Position 1: Stand with your weight evenly distributed and your back straight. Exhale, put your palms together in the 'prayer pose' (Fig. 8.1(a)).

Fig. 8.1(a)

Fig. 8.1(b)

Position 2: Inhale slowly and raise both arms upwards. Then start exhaling and bend downwards, touching the floor with both hands (Fig. 8.1(b)).

Position 3: Inhale, as you extend your left leg behind you, raise the head putting both hands on the floor (Fig. 8.1(c)).

Fig. 8.1(c)

Position 4: Stretch the right leg too and raise the body. Raise your hips so that your body forms an inverted 'V' (Fig. 8.1(d)).

Fig. 8.1(d)

Position 5: Lower your chest, touching the floor with your chin (Fig. 8.1(e)).

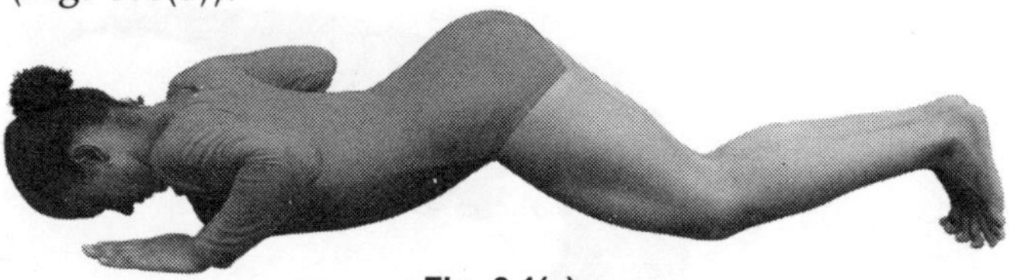

Fig. 8.1(e)

Position 6: Raise your head upwards. Also raise trunk, hips, thighs and knees from the floor (as in cobra pose) (Fig. 8.1(f)).

Fig. 8.1(f)

Position 7: The right foot is brought forward and left leg is stretched back (Fig. 8.1(g)).

Fig. 8.1(g)

Position 8: Raise the body with hands in the air (Fig. 8.1(h)).

Fig. 8.1(h)

Position 9: Join feet and bend backward, hands raised (Fig. 8.1(i)).

Fig. 8.1(i)

Fig. 8.1. Surya Namaskar

Position 10: Return to initial position with folded hands, standing erect (Fig. 8.1(a)).

Bhujang Asana

Also known as Cobra Posture. Lie on your stomach. Place your arms on sides of the chest. Inhale, raise your head and trunk slowly, leaning back as far as possible without raising the abdominal region (Fig. 8.2(a)). Hold for a few seconds. Exhale slowly (Fig. 8.2(b)). This asana helps to cure several female disorders and strengthen the muscles of breast (especially underdeveloped breasts).

(a)

(b)

Fig. 8.2. Bhujang Asana

Dhanur Asana

Fig. 8.3. Dhanur Asana

Also known as the Bow Posture. Lie on stomach. Keep your arms stretched on both sides. Rest the chin on the ground and take the ankles in hands. Now raise the legs, head and the upper part of the body while arching the back (Fig. 8.3). Remain in this position as long as possible. This asana tones up the muscles of breasts, abdominal organs, cures irregular or faulty menstruation, stimulates endocrine glands, prevents fat from forming around stomach and hips.

Gomukh Asana

Fig. 8.4. Gomukh Asana

Also known as the Cow Head Posture. Sit on the floor. Fold left leg in and right leg over the left leg so that one knee lies over the other. Take left arm on the back, placing left hand between the shoulder blades. Now take right hand behind on the back and hook fingers with the fingers of left hand (Fig. 8.4). Now interchange the position of your legs and arms. This posture strengthens the muscles of breasts, relieves cramps, tones up joint muscles, restores the synovial fluid, strengthen bones and especially helps bust development and strengthens the lungs and heart.

Vajroli Mudra

This posture is also known as the Boat Posture. This balancing pose (Fig. 8.5) strengthens the muscles of bust line, thighs and abdominal organs. It rids the digestive organs of toxins and helps to develop the sex will power in men and women between the age 25 to 40 years.

Fig. 8.5. Vajroli Mudra

Hal Asana (Plough Posture)

The feet are kept behind the head without bending the legs at the knees (Fig. 8.6). It gives good exercise to the back and bustline besides providing a glow to your face.

Fig. 8.6. Hal Asana

Supta Vajra Asana

Sit in Vajra Asana. Lie down on the back as shown in the illustration (Fig. 8.7). This asana strengthens the muscles of breast, back and legs.

Fig. 8.7. Supta Vajra Asana

Yoga Mudra

Sit in Padmasana. Now bend forward, keeping the forehead on the ground (Fig. 8.8). It presses the abdominal, breast and back muscles.

Fig. 8.8. Yoga Mudra

Natraj Asana

This posture is dedicated to Lord Shiva. This posture generates vigour, vitality, potency, flexibility to the limbs, shoulders, breasts and hips. Perform asana as shown in the illustration (Fig. 8.9).

Fig. 8.9. Natraj Asana

Stay in this position for eight to ten seconds and keep breathing normally. Perform posture on both legs, first left and then on right leg. Make four to six rounds daily. The posture leaves good effect upon the spine, enhances digestive power and improves eyesight.

Ushtra Asana

Sit on the floor. Fold the legs at the knees and keep them apart from one another at about six inches. Then stand on knees and bend towards back and catch hold of the back of the ankles (Fig. 8.10). Make the grip firm and stay for six to eight seconds.

Fig. 8.10. Ushtra Asana

Return to the initial position. Rest for six to eight seconds and bend the head and neck backwards again. Repeat for three to four times.

Ushtra Asana has several benefits. It corrects disorders of the neck, shoulders, breasts, spine and waist. It cures throat trouble, tonsil, voice defects and various types of visionary defects of the eyes. The posture enhances facial beauty.

9

Surgery for Diseases of Breast

Fatty tissue comprises a large part of the bulk of the breast. The breasts of prepubertal children consist entirely of ducts and connective tissues. At puberty, rudimentary gland buds increase in size and proliferate, the first manifestation of which is a symmetrical palpable enlargement or bud beneath the nipple. The full development requires about four years. During the reproductive years, the amount of fatty tissue increases alongwith the development of the lobular structure and fat to the glandular tissue which leaves a significant effect on the size and consistency of the breast. At puberty, the development of glandular tissue, the growth of duct system and the pigmentation of the areola and nipple are influenced by the rise in oestrogen levels.

The examination of female breast should be routine part of the physical examination of the gynaecologic patients. Pregnant women are not exempted from this examination. The breasts are inspected while the patient is seated without encumbering clothes or drapes with her hand clasped behind her head and her shoulders retracted. The presence of skin lesions, striae, erythema, increased vascularity, or abnormal development is noted.

The skin of breast is subject to the same types of disease as the skin elsewhere on the body. Small lesions such as nevi, warts, papillomas, hemangiomas, keratoses and furuncles, which seem obviously minor, may have a more serious connotation to the patient and should be noted in the record on breast diagram. More serious lesions like melanoma and Paget's disease must be biopsied. Prefer to wear correct size bra. On the inner or outer sides of the breast, deep strap marks indicate that the bra does not fit properly or is drawn too tight.

The left breast is often slightly larger than the right, but marked asymmetry rarely occurs. Variations in the size of normal breasts are a cause of concern to many women. The women whose breasts are seriously underdeveloped are candidated for augmentation mammoplasty. Women whose breasts are within the normal range should avoid having surgery. The fatty, heavy breasts of the perimenopausal or postmenopausal years may cause distressing psychological problems as well as discomfort in neck, back and shoulders from abnormal weight. Reduction mammoplasties afford great relief to these women. The breasts are palpated by gently squeezing them between the hands with the fingers perpendicular to the rib cage.

NIPPLE DISCHARGE

Among the more common causes of galactorrhoea are breast manipulation, sucking, or some form of athletic activity such as jogging. Improperly fitting garments may compress or inadequately support breasts, causing discharge. Other nipple secretions occur in a wide variety of colors and consistencies and are usually due to local disease. The nipple discharge is usually characteristically pale yellow, sticky and bilateral, usually there is no mass or tenderness present but the breast feels lumpy. It is advised to the patient to wear a carefully fitted garment and avoid undue constraint or friction. Every woman should perform monthly examinations of her breast postmenstrually, when the breast is least engorged. The factors affecting risk predisposing to breast carcinoma include family history, advancing age, carcinoma in other breast, precancerous mastopathy, early puberty, late age at first childbirth, late menopause, western culture, irradiation and other carcinoma of colon, uterus and ovary. Other risk factors are exogenous oestrogen, nutrition, obesity, breastfeeding and high parity. The diagnostic aids in the management of breast disease include mammography, thermography, ultrasonography, diaphanography and nuclear magnetic resonance.

SURGERY FOR DISEASES OF BREAST

Palpable discrete or dominant lumps in the breast must be surgically investigated after mammography, even if the latter is negative. When the mass is rounded, well circumscribed, smooth and 1 cm or greater in diameter, it is probably a cyst or fibro-adenoma, and ultrasound can differentiate between the two. Aspiration should be attempted first. With the patient lying supine in a relaxed position, the mass is stabilized with the thumb and first two fingers of the left hand (Fig. 9.1(a)). Local anesthesia is undesirable in the tissue to be aspirated. A needle (No. 22) attached to a syringe (20-cc) is passed tangentially into the mass while suction is maintained (Fig. 9.1(b)). If the lesion is cystic, the light brown fluid obtained usually flows freely in the syringe. This fluid is sent to the laboratory for cytologic evaluation. If no fluid is obtained after several attempts, the needle is withdrawn and whatever obtained material is sent for cytologic analysis. Cysts smaller in size than 1 cm are difficult to aspirate. If one of these is such lesion, it should be treated by open biopsy. Insert needle perpendicularly to the chest wall, rather than at an angle of 30 to 40 degree.

When a solid mass is present, a multiple aspiration technique is attempted (Fig. 9.1(c)), preferably without local anesthesia. To avoid bringing the aspirated material into the syringe, suction is discontinued before the needle is pulled back through

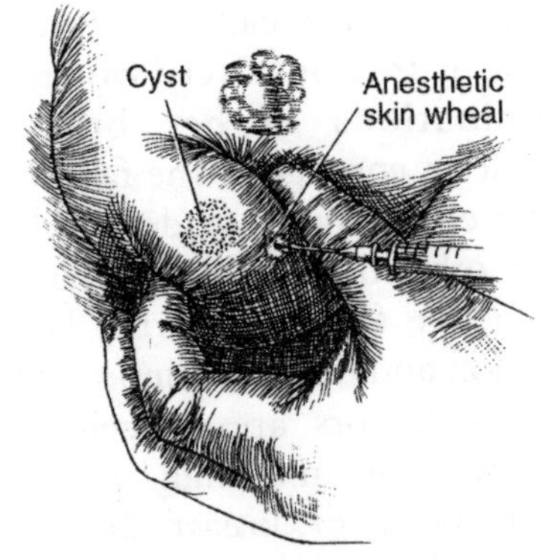

Fig. 9.1(a). Small intradermal wheal raised over cyst

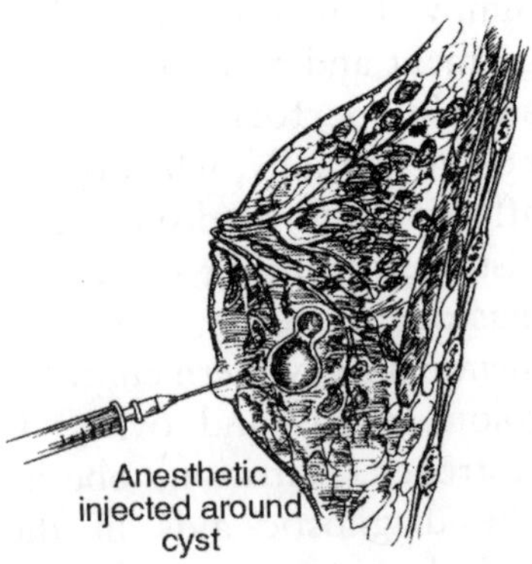

Fig. 9.1(b). Injection of anesthesia

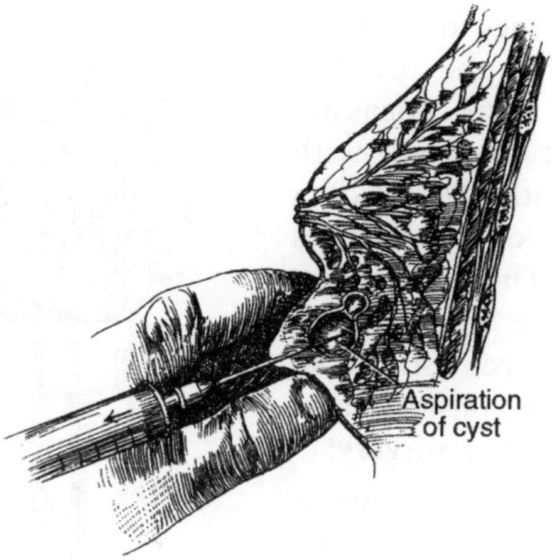

Fig. 9.1(c). Portion of breast containing the cyst is stabilized

the skin. The procedure is repeated five or six times. Each of these aspirations should be done quickly to avoid contamination of the specimen using local anesthesia. Skinny needle (No. 22) is passed repeatedly through the lesion in different planes and directions by means of syringe holder. The aspirate is ejected on a slide and sent for cytologic analysis (Fig. 9.1(d) & (e)). A high

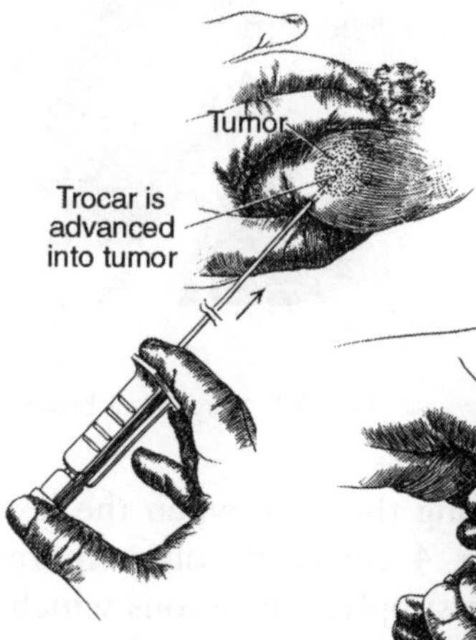

Fig. 9.1(d)

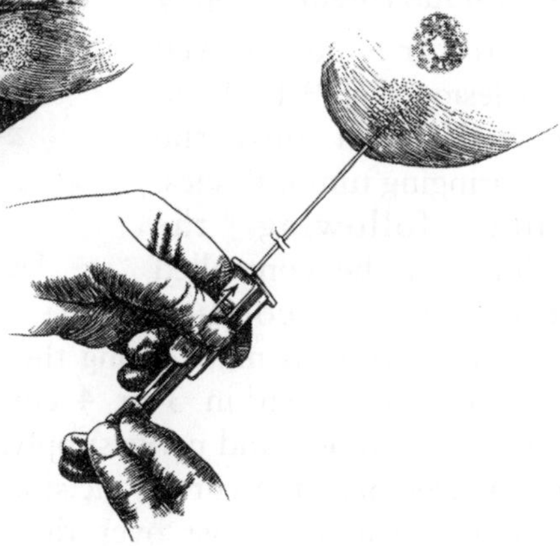

Fig. 9.1(e)

degree of accuracy in diagnosis is possible, but the result is not definitive as specimens are usually contaminated with blood. A negative report on a suspicious lesion necessitates tissue biopsy. The figure shows the functioning of a syringe holder. Positive aspiration findings may be considered for initiating definitive surgery.

Small biopsy specimens can be obtained by the percutaneous passage of a trocar containing a cutting needle. The cutting edge of the trocar is pushed into the breast tissue by giving local anesthesia. An open biopsy is indicated in the case of a mass, a bloody nipple discharge, retracted nipple or skin area or a positive mammograms.

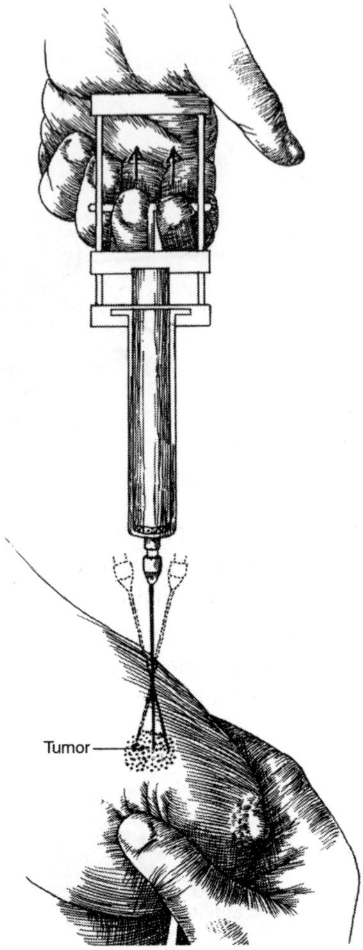

(f)

Fig. 9.1. Surgery of breast

Percutaneous Needle Biopsy

The trocar is pushed well into the lesion (Fig. 9.1(f)) and then withdrawn into the sheath, bringing tumor tissues. Bleeding following the procedure can be controlled by pressure. To conduct biopsy, the incision is made along the edge when the lesion is beneath the areola within 3 or 4 cm of its outer margin to compromise its blood and nerve supply. For lesions which exist deep in a large breast, a curved incision 3 or 4 cm long is made parallel to the areolar just over the lesion as shown in the figures.

The surgeon explores the location of the lesion with his or her forefinger. If the lesion is not directly beneath the incision, it is necessary to tunnel toward it with scissors, pushing, spreading and cutting towards the desired location. The surgeon usually has better understanding of assessing the size and nature of the lesion. The lesions less than 4 cm in diameter and probably malignant should be sharply excised with a surrounding margin of normal tissue (Fig. 9.2(a) & (b)). Once the decision has been made to excise the lesion, the surgeon grasps the tissue overlying the lesion with small curved scissors and tooth forceps (Fig. 9.2(c), (d) & (e)). After removal of the tumor, the defect is closed with fine suture material (Fig. 9.2(f)). The bleeding should be controlled before closure and a pressure dressing is applied.

When a bloody nipple discharge suggests the likelihood of an intraductal papilloma, sharp dissection is carried from a circumareolar incision placed in the breast quadrant. A generous portion of the duct system around the diseased area is resected, and the severed ends are ligated. The Fig. 9.3 shows incisional

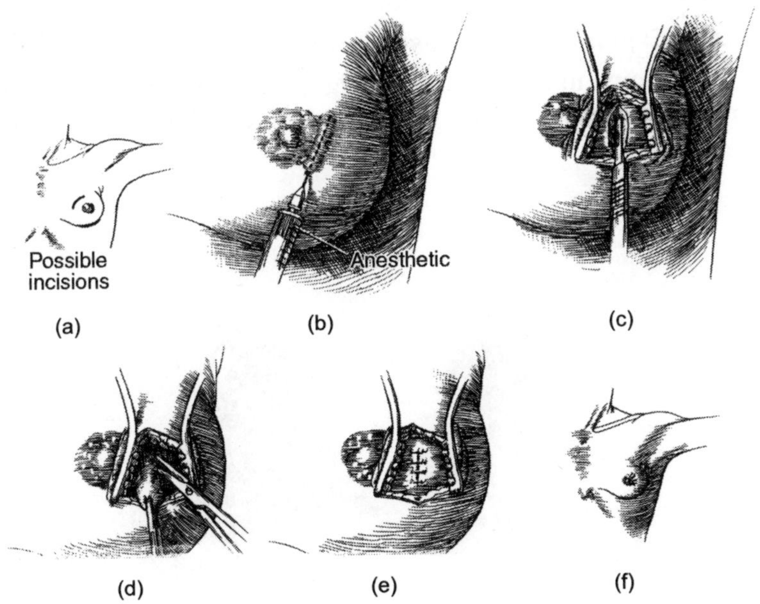

Fig. 9.2. Removal of tumor

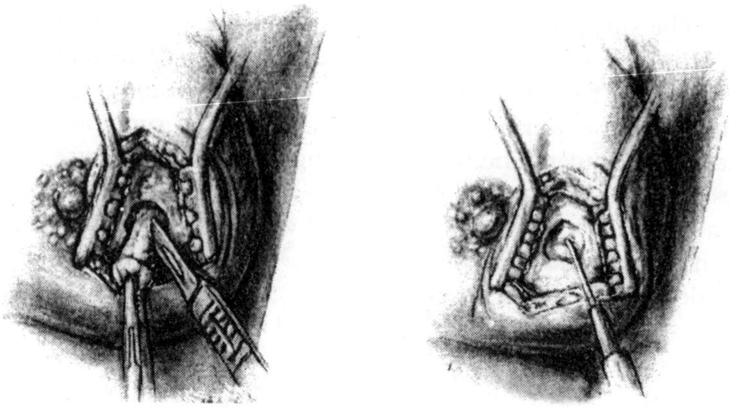

(a) (b)

Fig. 9.3. Incisional biospy

biopsy. The Fig. 9.3(a) indicates when a large (over 5 cm) lesion is encountered, especially when carcinoma is strongly suspected. The Fig. 9.3(b) is the base of the incision, which is usually coagulated to control bleeding.

Ductal Exploration and Resection of Papilloma

As shown in Fig. 9.4 below, Fig. (a) indicates the incision is circumareolar and toward the quadrant most likely to be the site

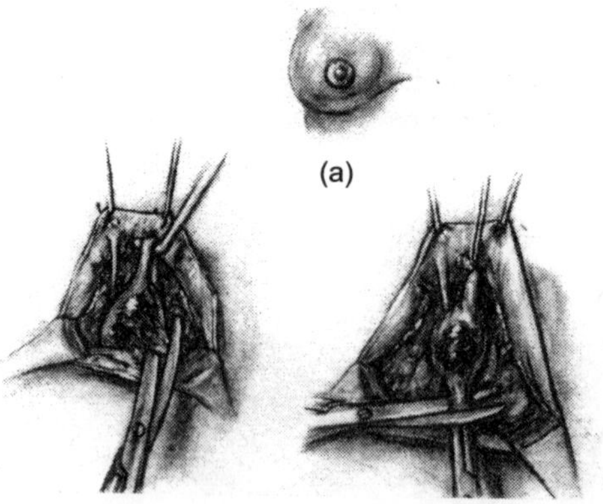

(a)

(b) (c)

Fig. 9.4. Ductal exploration and resection of papilloma

of the lesion. With traction on the main duct, peripheral branches are dissected out until the lesion is identified as shown in Fig. (b). The Fig. (c) shows the duct system above and below the lesion is clamped.

Biopsy of Non-palpable Lesions

The direction of incision should be downward to the intersection of the flexible hook in the vicinity of the lesion as shown in Fig. 9.5. An appropriate volume of tissue around it is being undermined. The lesion with at least 1 cc of surrounding tissue, is resected and verified radiologically and pathologically. If the lesion is not identified in the specimen by X-ray, an additional volume of tissue must be resected.

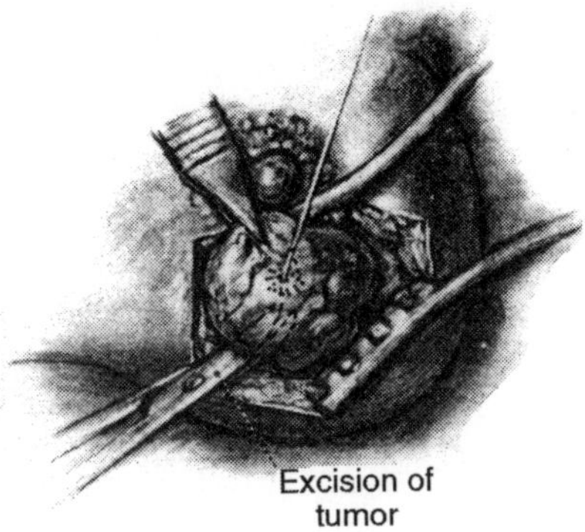

Fig. 9.5. Biopsy of non-palpable lesions

Axillary Lymph Node Dissection

This should be done by an experienced surgeon under general anesthesia. The surgery can be done as a second stage operation following conservative resection of the primary tumor. A diagonal incision is made across the base of the axilla from the edge of the pectoralis major as shown in Fig. 9.6. This incision should be separate from the incision in the breast. The axillary vein is exposed by incising the

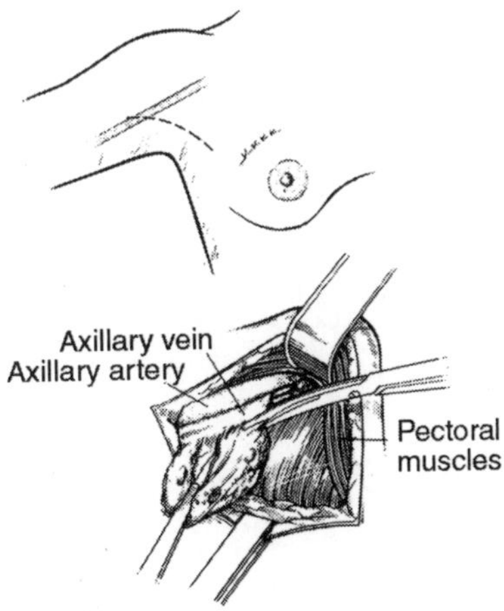

Fig. 9.6. Axillary lymph node dissection

costocoracoid fascia. The fatty tissue and enclosed lymphatics beneath the vein are carefully dissected. Following excision of the lump that showed carcinoma, top breast incision is closed. Currently, augmentation mammoplasty is used, in which the incision may be made beneath the breast which leaves an invisible scar.